D0943726

# The Embattled Fortress

*Joseph E. Izzo*

# The Embattled Fortress

## *Strategies for Restoring Information Systems Productivity*

Jossey-Bass Publishers

San Francisco  •  London  •  1987

THE EMBATTLED FORTRESS
*Strategies for Restoring Information Systems Productivity*
by Joseph E. Izzo

Copyright © 1987 by: Jossey-Bass Inc., Publishers
433 California Street
San Francisco, California 94104
&
Jossey-Bass Limited
28 Banner Street
London EC1Y 8QE

**Library of Congress Cataloging-in-Publication Data**

Izzo, Joseph E., date.
  The embattled fortress.

  (The Jossey-Bass management series)
  Bibliography: p.
  Includes index.
    1. Business—Data processing.  2. Management—
Data processing.  3. Information technology.
I. Title. II. Series.
HF5548.3.197   1987      658.4'038      87-45429
ISBN 1-55542-059-1 (alk. paper)

Manufactured in the United States of America

The paper in this book meets the guidelines for
permanence and durability of the Committee on
Production Guidelines for Book Longevity of the
Council on Library Resources.


JACKET DESIGN BY WILLI BAUM




FIRST EDITION

*Code 8729*

*The Jossey-Bass Management Series*

A special thanks
to Mary Troyer
for her effort in the development
of this book.

# Contents

ix

# Preface

*The Embattled Fortress: Strategies for Restoring Information Systems Productivity* is not a computer book, nor is it a management book. It does not explain computer principles, what computers can do, or how to use them. It is a book about business technology as a *resource* and how business should view and use that resource in order to achieve the elusive "competitive edge." It is also about people who work with computers, information systems professionals, the users of computers, and executive management, all of whom ardently desire a solution to their information systems predicament.

     The information systems department is under siege in corporate America today because it has not lived up to its promise of increasing productivity and contributing to business's goals in the marketplace. As an organization, it resists change. It creates constraints and hurdles that stifle and impair innovation. Instead of seeking new ways to increase the availability of computer technology throughout the business, it often thwarts them. All this and more has turned information systems into an embattled fortress. If this situation is to improve, senior management must be able to converse knowledgeably and constructively with information systems professionals. Management must see results and value for the vast amount of money spent on computer hardware, software, and services. Users must overcome their mistrust and resentment of information systems—and information systems itself must become an enthusiastic partner in helping the firm meet its goals.

The concepts brought forward in this book apply to all information technologies—business systems, telecommunications, office automation, robotics, artificial intelligence, electronic publishing, and any other application that uses the computer as the core delivery mechanism.

While this book is written for people in management, it differs from the vast majority of books on management problems in that it offers no quick fixes, no short-term solutions to the computer problem. It does what no other book in the marketplace does: In plain language, using concrete examples from actual business situations, it addresses a critical problem: We're trying to use steam-engine methods to run space-age companies. *The Embattled Fortress* proposes that the warring parties sit down and air their differences and, with that done, begin working together, as they have never done before, to solve the problems facing the firm. There can be no lasting, meaningful change in the way technology is used unless and until people start to change, and change is what this book is all about.

*The Embattled Fortress: Strategies for Restoring Information Systems Productivity* is for the reader who has come away from the fad books still wanting more. This book is for chief executives who have reached their wit's end with the information systems organization. It is for the senior managers who know things must change if the company is to move aggressively ahead, but who need guidance on how or where to start. It is for information systems executives or managers who want to reposition the computer technology, but who know that more computers or disk drives is not the answer. And it is for all the managers in marketing, manufacturing, engineering, or the information center, as well as managers in the public sector and in government, who want to get more out of the firm's computers but need help in formulating the correct strategy.

The problems, the strategies, and the solutions I describe

in this book come from my thirty-odd years in business. I have spent the past ten years working with senior management all across the country, practicing what this book espouses. This is not academic theory, nor is it simply my opinion or vision of what ought to be. It's the real world of American business today. I have worked with real companies in the real world for too long to believe that one solution works for everyone, or that problems dating back as much as twenty years can be solved overnight. This book, then, should be used as a guide in your quest to find your own best strategy to solve your particular information systems problems.

This book is organized into three main sections. Part One offers an overview of the computer culture and how past events have led to today's problems. Chapter One asks, Is the computer enhancing productivity? Is it providing information for better management decision making? There are only three criteria for deciding to use a computer: Will we be able to do it cheaper, faster, or better? Improvement of productivity should be the determining factor. Computer technology is an enabling device that should be used to enhance the firm's strategic position or competitive advantage. Chapter Two discusses the identity crisis the information systems department has undergone because it doesn't know what it's supposed to do for the firm and lacks direction to get on track. Moreover, information systems has failed to make the technological transition necessary to provide useful computing services for a modern business.

Chapter Three explains that, as business practices have changed over the past thirty years, our ways of utilizing the computer resource have not. This chapter discusses such common myths as centralized computing, the need for more and bigger computers, and the so-called incompetent user, and dispels them. Chapter Four reveals that in the early days of computers, users were largely technologically deficient, yet out of that group the knowledge user emerged, who understands how technology works. This chapter discusses the impact of the personal computer and the rise of knowledge users. But it also goes on to describe a whole new class of user that is emerging:

the enlightened user, who does not necessarily understand technical nuances but who does know how to make computers work to meet business goals.

Part Two begins by describing actions we can take now to begin turning the situation around. Chapter Five explains where the notion of centralized computing came from and shows how, over the past forty years, business has moved from centralized, industrial-age tenets to more modern, individualistic practices. This is why we see microcomputers throughout the firm today. True productivity gains will only come when computer power is dispersed—placed in the hands of the users. Chapter Six explains that although planning tomorrow's dispersed computer architecture is not difficult, there must be a formal plan. A dispersed architecture puts computers and their applications where they are most useful, while the central computing facility retains its important functions. All this can be done gradually, in stages, without extensive capital outlay. Chapter Seven explains that implementing a dispersed architecture involves more than hardware and software. It involves people, too, and the way to effect true change is by forming a "skunk works" style committee to conceive and develop the strategy and the plans for the new computer systems architecture.

Part Three provides management with ideas and strategies for repositioning and redirecting the energies of their information systems organization. Chapter Eight explains the importance of solving today's problems, and at the same time building tomorrow's information systems environment. The mission of the information systems organization is to ensure that computing services meet the firm's goals for success in the future. Chapter Nine points out that one of the major foundations of yesterday's embattled fortress—control policies for dispersing computers and computer services throughout the business—must be reexamined. New creative methods of control must be developed that allow greater freedom in computer use, while exercising responsible management of this vital resource. Chapter Ten presents the importance of executive management involvement in achieving productive use of computer technology within a business. It details how this involvement should take place and how business leadership can create a strong relationship between the direction of information systems and business objectives.

The Epilogue, "Challenging the Status Quo," elucidates what is needed to turn your information systems organization around. What is that? In a word, courage. The key is a willingness to take the risks inherent in implementing a new computer architecture and the strategies necessary to get all the appropriate people involved and working together to do it. Strategy is something small, not something complicated and grand. A good strategy creates a winning situation for all the players. It is a way of thinking about things, an idea that I stress again and again in this book.

*Santa Monica, California*                                          Joseph E. Izzo
*August 1987*

# Acknowledgments

I would like to thank the people who, over the years, have challenged and stimulated me to embark upon this quest. They have influenced my thinking, stirred my reflections, and moved me to make changes in direction. They have vividly reminded me that computers are essential in achieving success in business. They have helped me realize that computers must be looked at differently and that data processing must service corporations differently than in the past.

These are leaders who don't allow the computer, information systems, or the computer manufacturers to dictate how computers are used in their corporations. They are becoming key orchestrators in determining how computers will be used in the future. They are:

James A. Collins, chairman, and Richard Bermingham, chief executive officer, Collins Foods International, Inc.

Larry R. DeJarnett, vice-president, Information Systems, Lear-Siegler, Inc.

Joseph T. Gallagher, vice-president and general manager, Aircraft Division, Northrop Corporation

James H. Kogen, president, Shure Brothers, Inc.

Emil P. Martini, Jr., chairman and chief executive officer, Bergen-Brunswig Corporation

DuWayne J. Peterson, executive vice-president, Merrill Lynch & Co., Inc.

Sanford C. Sigoloff, chairman, chief executive officer, and president, the Wickes Companies, Inc.

Hugh Brady, former general manager and vice-president at TRW Space and Technology, deserves a special acknowledgment. He is a visionary who saw that computers kept in isolation could never become available to the operating people, those who truly make a difference and a profit in the business. While at TRW, Brady began working on their new system architecture. He created the Levels of Maximum Management (LOMM) concept, which moved the levels of computer capability out to the users where it made a genuine difference.

I also thank the following people who graciously consented to be interviewed during the preparation of this book: Ira S. Gottfried, CMC, executive partner, Management Consulting Services, Coopers and Lybrand; Alex Pantaleoni, director of the Administration of Justice Program, Rio Hondo College; Arthur J. Peever, president, Arrowhead Drinking Water, Beatrice Foods Bottled Water Division; Robert E. Umbaugh, president, Mission Land Company (a subsidiary of Southern California Edison Company); and Patricia Walker, vice-president, Gannett Outdoor of Southern California.

An acknowledgment goes to many of the JIA Management Group, Inc., staff, who have been instrumental in developing these concepts and implementing them in the real world. A special thanks to Maurice D. Pratt, a founder of JIA, whose work with our clients helped formulate many of the architecture ideas discussed in this book. And I would like to thank my colleague, able writer Jack B. Rochester, for guiding me through the intricacies of writing this book.

I have long admired the art of Rockwell Kent and have been permitted to use his works in many of my company's materials. I chose *Beowulf and the Dragon* for this book. I am grateful to the Rockwell Kent Legacies, Sally Kent Gorton, director, for permission to use this illustration.

J. E. I.

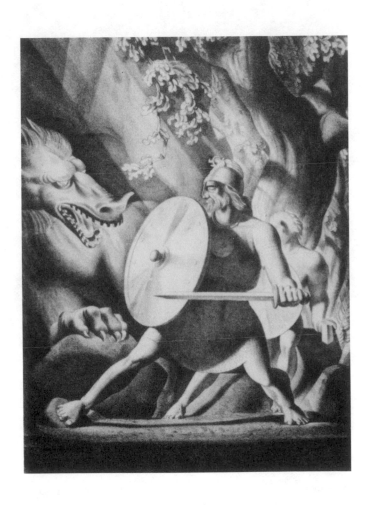

# The Author

Joseph E. Izzo has spent his entire professional life on the leading edge of computer technology and business management. Since 1976, he has been president and chief executive officer of the JIA Management Group, Inc., in Santa Monica, California.

Since 1953, Izzo has worked in every aspect of computer information systems, from programming to senior management. He was a systems designer/programmer for the U.S. Air Force's SAGE (Semi-Automatic Ground Environment) air defense computer, which set the standards for many other computer systems to follow. He has worked at Columbus and Southern Ohio Electric, System Development Corporation (a "think tank" that evolved from the Rand Corporation), and Rocketdyne (a division of North American Rockwell).

Under Izzo's direction, the Rocketdyne information systems facility became one of the largest and most advanced in the nation. It was IBM's showcase operation, and computer scientists and engineers came from around the world to tour the facility.

He left to assume a vice-presidency in the commercial division of Computer Sciences Corporation, the world's largest independent professional computer services company in the computer industry.

Izzo's cumulative experience convinced him that most firms could profit from improving information systems' contribution to business goals. Thus was born what Izzo terms turnaround management, the concept of bringing a team of professionals into an information systems organization to restore productivity and improve efficiency.

Turnaround management and future strategies that develop information systems effectiveness are the keystones of Izzo's firm, the JIA Management Group, Inc., a thirty-person management consulting firm. This unique concept, which no other management consulting firm offers, as well as Izzo's thoughts and views, have been the subject of articles in such periodicals as the *Wall Street Journal, Management Technology,* the *Los Angeles Times, Computerworld,* and *Datamation,* among others.

The Embattled Fortress

# Introduction

## The Quest
## for Information Systems
## Productivity

This book is about the embattled fortress, the term I use to describe today's beleaguered information systems department. It is a quest for answers to the many problems we all face with information systems. It is a search for the real causes that block our ability to restructure information systems to fulfill the competitive needs of business. It is a quest for solutions that will allow the computer to meet the performance goals that we demand in business.

A quest requires time and patience to achieve the desired results. Business executives and information systems executives must work patiently together with the shared belief that they can make the necessary changes. This search demands a major shift in thinking and a willingness to penetrate the cultural frameworks that have developed over many years. Once we understand these factors, we will be in a much better position to change them and improve our business's performance.

The computer and its problems represent an area that many businesses would like to sweep under the carpet. The technology is difficult to understand. It is hard to communicate

1

with technically minded data processing personnel. Information systems budgets continually rise, with no observable improvement in services. Many executives know what they would like their computers to do, but have difficulty getting the information systems to understand their requests. (In this book, when I use the term "information systems," I am referring to a company's information systems *department.*) Information systems seems to be growing larger, more difficult to manage, and less effective with each passing day.

Consider this comment from the general manager at an aircraft manufacturing firm:

> You people in data processing keep telling me about all the money the company is going to save by adding more computer capability. Well, five years ago we were building six hundred tons of aircraft, we employed ten thousand people, and our computer costs were $24 million a year. This year we are building six hundred tons of aircraft, we have eleven thousand employees, and our computer costs are $70 million a year. Please explain to me more clearly how the computer is saving us money.

Or consider this comment from the president of an electronics distribution company: "The computer response time and system availability are so bad that we are losing business to our competitors to the tune of $200,000 a day."

What has gone wrong? Has the information systems organization forgotten its mission? Faced with its inability to satisfy user demands and enhance the firm's productivity, information systems has retreated. As an organization, it resents the users' implications of poor performance. Instead of seeking new, innovative ways to support the firm, it all too often stifles and suppresses them. The net result is that other organizations resent information systems and often attempt football-style end runs to avoid dealing with it. All this has turned information systems into an embattled fortress.

The problem is not without a solution. Those firms with a strong, focused information systems organization will thrive and succeed in the 1980s and 1990s. How?

Computer technology must be integrated into the firm's mission and goals, from initial planning through product delivery and service. Many business managers and executives sense this, but they do not know how to orchestrate the necessary changes.

What kinds of changes are needed? First, a change in *how we think* about computers. The fact is, business has been changing dramatically over the past thirty years. We no longer operate under the tenets of the Industrial Age. The business world of today is abuzz over international trade, the factory of the future, new market segments, and of course, computers.

Unfortunately, the people who run the computers have not been able to keep pace with changes in business practices. Basic computer systems architecture has not changed since the design of the first commercial computer. Most of the programs and applications in use today are ten to fifteen years old. Our leading-edge technology is sadly lagging.

I am convinced that the future belongs to the firm with the most efficient, businesslike information systems practices. Yet if we are going to renew the promise of computer productivity and take those strides into the future, we must first tear down the walls of the embattled fortress. This does not demand firing the information systems staff, nor does it necessarily require new computer systems to replace the old.

Instead, we must first ask some very serious questions about information systems. What is the role of information systems in the firm? What can computers do to help the business operate more efficiently and profitably? The questions and answers will challenge some basic assumptions about information systems and how we have been using computers in our businesses.

But if we are going to get what we want, we must be willing to strive for it. This means that senior management—and information systems management and the management of user groups—must make a commitment and take an active role in effecting the necessary changes. This is, after all, a quest. It holds the promise of great returns, but it is not without risk. It requires a strong will and a deep commitment, yet the rewards are there for the successful.

*The Embattled Fortress: Strategies for Restoring Information Systems Productivity* is not a panacea. There is no one correct path to the solution. Readers must ultimately find the best path for their companies. I challenge you to join the quest for solutions to your information systems problems. Together, I am certain we can overcome this crisis and restore the lost promise of computer productivity.

# PART ONE

# Today's Information Systems Environment

The way things are done in the current information systems environment is the way things have been done since the mid-1960s. But the old ways are no longer working. We face a choice: We can continue applying computer technology to business in these old ways and accept the consequences, or we can challenge some of these basic tenets, and thus learn to manage this valuable resource much better.

To create change within a culture or environment, we must first understand what exists and how it works. In order to challenge current systems and procedures and create new directions, we must be clear on what does not work. Without this basic understanding, there can be no real change. Chapters One through Four deal with these issues.

# 1

⊓⊔⊓⊔⊓⊔⊓⊔⊓⊔⊓⊔⊓⊔⊓⊔⊓⊔⊓⊔⊓⊔⊓⊔⊓⊔⊓⊔⊓⊔⊓⊔⊓⊔⊓⊔⊓⊔⊓⊔

# Paradise Lost: Promises of Information Systems Productivity

For many years now, the computer industry's clarion call (also taken up by hardware manufacturers and software publishers) has been, This is the latest computer technology. Without it, you are at a disadvantage. And this call (picked up by information systems organizations) has echoed in the corporate halls: We must have this new technology. We must be the leaders. We must be the first to acquire the latest technology, regardless of the cost.

And, for over thirty years, business leaders have assented to these demands, hoping for productivity gains that have yet to materialize. Yet there is still an almost frantic rush to automate. Whenever a task is performed there is, more often than not, the immediate question: Can we put it on the computer? We are caught in a self-propagating spiral that says computers are good, that there should be one on every desk, and that they should be used for almost any task.

There is no question that computers are here to stay. They grow more accepted, and more commonplace, with each passing day. However, this should in no way diminish our expectations or our demand that they provide demonstrable benefits that accrue to the business as a whole. To automate simply because it seems like the thing to do, or because the rest of the world is doing it, is not a sufficient reason. First, we must understand what the computer does well. Then we must ask ourselves if it lends itself to the task at hand. Finally, we must ask if the computer, performing that particular task, provides any productivity improvement for the business.

How often do you hear people talk about how computer technology should be helping their businesses? How many managers take the trouble to ask: What is automation going to do for my bottom line? Or: Will the computer help to produce my product better, faster, or cheaper? Or: What will the computer do to help my firm achieve its goals?

Computer costs are certain, but benefits are not. In fact, computers may go down as the most oversold technology since the zeppelin. In my view, automation is becoming technology for technology's sake. This is just plain irresponsible.

When we consider building a new plant, adding a new sales territory, or making a new product, we usually ask, What are the benefits? We also ask how this additional expense will increase our profits or help our growth. Yet how many corporations continue to increase their information systems budgets from 6 to 20 percent a year, year after year, on something for which the measurable return cannot be identified or tracked? The computer investment is a risk, just like a new plant, a new sales territory, or any other investment. Why take this risk with virtually no assurance of return or gain? Do we need to take this risk at all?

And if we do, we must look beyond the price of the computer hardware. We must subject proposed computer *applications* to a cost–benefit–risk analysis, for it is the applications that eventually prompt additional hardware acquisitions. Moreover, it is the application, running on the hardware, that either benefits the business or has no impact whatsoever.

It just makes good business sense to ask these kinds of questions before developing new computer applications or purchasing new computers and peripherals. The benefits can be, and must be, measurable and quantifiable. There is no reason the added expense cannot contribute to the bottom line and, ultimately, to the company's growth.

## The Leading-Edge Tool

The computer is the United States' leading-edge technological development. It has been heralded as the device that will help business achieve and enhance its productivity goals. The United States created the technology that the rest of the world buys, licenses, mimics, and emulates. Therefore, we cannot accept the position that we are not using it to our own competitive advantage. We are mired in old systems, in old uses of the equipment, and in old ways of doing things—we must extricate ourselves from this mess.

It is time to take a closer look at how we apply computer technology in business and government. It is not satisfactory to take a manual process (such as order entry) and fill in the blanks on a computer screen instead of on a piece of paper, and then claim that this is faster. Rather than use computers to simply speed things up, we need to think of how we can use them to perform tasks differently, more efficiently, and more intelligently than we do today.

One of my clients, the president of a prominent high-fidelity electronics manufacturing firm, found that the approach to automation in his business had become a key inhibitor to his company reaching its goals. He wanted to make changes in his business processes to remain competitive in his industry, but information systems was unable to make corresponding modifications in the computer systems. (In this book, when I refer to information systems, I am referring to a company's information systems *department.*) To his consternation, he found yesterday's processes indelibly implanted in his computer systems. No matter how he attempted to change the business processes, the computers prevented anything more than minor restructuring.

This client was convinced the way his company did business required significant alteration. He was equally convinced that change could not happen using the current computer system. The system was holding his company back; it was telling him how to conduct his business rather than the other way around.

This president decided that the only way to meet his industry's competitive situation (and thus achieve success in the future) was to get rid of the old computer systems and install new ones. To be sure, this is not the answer for every company with information systems problems. But the important thing is that the man *thought* about the problems, and then made the decision to *change* things. Had he simply given up and accepted the status quo, he would have lost his competitive edge.

Consider the federal government. It is the world's largest computer user and computer services provider, yet no one can tell you how productive—or profitable—its agencies are. We assume that most of those agencies try to do their best, but there is no measuring tool. It is ludicrous that the Veterans Administration pays out $15 billion a year in benefits, but makes mistakes in computerized payment records that total over $500 million annually. Poorly computerized accounting practices make it nearly impossible to track government loans, resulting in $35 billion in past-due payments at the end of 1982. Social-program directors have no way to verify poverty aid recipients' incomes, so overpayments totaling $4 billion a year are made.

The computer is not providing the support for either government or business to be more productive and competitive, yet we are buying computers right and left. According to International Data Corporation, a market research firm, in 1986—generally considered a slow year for the industry—U.S. corporations bought well over 3 million desktop computers.* That was over 25 percent more than the year before. Yet during a company tour with one of my clients, I saw office after office filled with idle machines. He told me the firm had purchased $35 million worth of desktop microcomputers, yet it appeared that most of them were sitting unused, and people were spending a lot of time trying to figure out what to do with them.

---

*J. Peter Grace. *Burning Money: The Waste of Your Tax Dollars* (New York: Macmillan, 1984), p. 133.

Why has this occurred? Are we buying computers simply to have more computers? Have we lost sight of the reason we are in business? Has the information systems department forsaken its mission to improve the firm's efficiency and profitability by automating its functions?

The computer industry has oversold the computer for its own purposes: namely, to sell more computers. It has told business that it must have computers or else. That is certainly wrong, yet business has bought into it. Business has been intimidated into adding another cost of doing business without a reciprocal benefit. Today's information systems departments have enough computing power to achieve a huge leap in productivity. Unfortunately, computers have become a kind of business amoeba, propagating in the halls of corporations and government agencies while giving little in return.

Do not misunderstand. I believe the computer can enhance business and help meet the challenges of the marketplace. It is a powerful tool for innovation, for new product development, and for determining new markets. But equally important, the computer is capable of helping the firm deliver high-quality products at a competitive price. In order to do so, however, we must clearly understand what the computer can do, as well as what it cannot.

### What Is Wrong, and How Can We Make It Right?

We have seen dramatic changes in management concepts and styles since the 1960s. The role of workers is under debate as they are given greater autonomy to manage their own affairs within the framework of the business's overall goals. The marketplace continues to change and evolve, and the time span in which we can respond to change has shortened considerably.

Even with all these changes in business, information systems practices have changed very little. Why? The computer and its application structures are products of Industrial Age thinking. The machine was designed in the 1940s, and remains basically unchanged. The applications structures were established in the 1950s and 1960s, forming the basis for every application since then. It is difficult for a massive, highly structured data base application created in 1970 to respond adequately in today's dynamic, fast-paced business environment. Even the new systems are designed using yesterday's rigid specifications. This precludes all but minimal changes for supporting contemporary business requirements.

To make matters worse, information systems is getting further and further behind each year in its ability to respond to the business's changing needs. One of the primary reasons for this is the concept of centralized computing as we know it today. It is blocking the information systems department's ability to support the productivity and competitive needs of the business. What is needed is a radical change in approach: hardware distribution, systems design philosophy, even the organization of the information systems department must be revised and revitalized to support the business.

*Perils of the Information Age.* Over the past few years, both business generally and the computer industry specifically have embraced the concept of the "Information Age." This highly touted phenomenon promises easy access to reports, statistics, facts, and a host of other materials, ostensibly bestowing the King Midas touch on corporate goals. College textbooks teach students *"information* resource management" or "management *information* systems." "Decision support systems" software promises to combine information resources so users can make strategic decisions for the firm.

All this talk has led many to believe that information is itself an end product of the computer. We've been led to believe that information has value—that it will lead us from ignorance to knowledge. This view of the importance of information, promulgated by people in the computer industry or the information systems department, is essentially self-serving. It is an attempt to make something more of the computer's output than is really there.

There is nothing wrong with information; it's just that computers do not produce it. They produce *data.* It is when a human being takes the computer's data and passes it through a cognitive, mental process that we get *information.* The human then uses that information to make a decision, hopefully for the good of the firm.

The president of a restaurant chain challenged the value of a new computer system his information systems staff was installing. It was intended to tie the cash registers at 250 restaurants into a central computer. One of the system's purposes was to extract summary information, monitor restaurant performance, and maintain cash control on a daily basis. In addition, the system would, according to information systems, extract "information" on what menu items in the current advertising campaign were selling.

As the details of the system were being hammered out, the president asked a very incisive question: Why do we need data from all 250 restaurants to determine the effectiveness of our advertising campaigns? Why don't we just take a sampling of representative locations? After heated discussions, the conclusion was that data from twenty restaurants would be 95 percent accurate in determining the ad campaign's effectiveness.

This settled, the discussion turned back to the daily data-gathering. The president again asserted himself by telling information systems that he did not want the detailed data generated in the 250 restaurants to be stored in a central file. Not only would the cost of computer processing and storage be excessive, but there would be a human tendency to find other ways to use the data if it were available. This, in turn, would result in countless hours spent on tasks that "could be better used improving the bottom line," in the president's words. Further, "Restaurant managers know what *is* and what *is not* selling in their restaurants, and are fully capable of adjusting accordingly. They do not need the help of the back room poring over hundreds of pages of data to tell them what to do."

Information is an essential ingredient in business. It gives us insight, the ability to see clearly, to understand, and the ability to achieve goals we might not otherwise achieve. But all this talk about the Information Age neglects the fact that a product or a service is the goal, and that information is only one aspect of achieving that goal. Information is not the goal itself. This president understood that whatever else we do with either data or information, the number-one goal was to make sure the business is a high-quality, cost-competitive producer. Far too often the Information Age is getting in the way of our viewing the computer as a device for operating a business more efficiently. In other words, it's creating the wrong focus.

Hugh Brady, former general manager at TRW, put it this way: "Information is a nonproduct. Whatever you're doing in this world, information is an adjunct to it, and not an end in itself. Of course, there are companies in the business of providing information. They have established that information is their product, and I have no quarrel with them. What I am talking about are businesses that produce automobiles, airplanes, television sets, and other goods. What they produce are physical, tangible things. I am concerned about what my business sells, my competition, the latest quality innovations, product life spans, and my customers' needs. I do need information, but it is information about my product that has the most meaning" (interview, June 27, 1985).

The information systems department must clearly understand that its role is to build systems that solve business problems and help achieve corporate goals. Information is an essential by-product of any process, but the end goal is developing more efficient automation processes for the operation of the business.

Mr. Brady tells the story this way: "A few years ago, our data processing department was called management information systems, so instead of selling just data processing services they were selling management information systems. Here I was, a user, so I said OK, I need a new management system for my operations.

"Well, instead of sending me someone who could analyze how I was running my *business,* they sent me programmers who analyzed my *organization.* They computerized the system I had, but they didn't give me a better system. They expanded the system by searching out all the data intersections, and I wound up with more data than I ever knew existed or cared about.

"Finally I said, 'Do you know what we are doing? We're

taking my organization as it is and pouring it into the concrete of the computer. You come in and spend a considerable amount of time and money, and all I have is more information. You're trying to computerize something that wasn't operating right in the first place. Go away, and I'll determine what type of system I need and how I really want to operate in this world. Then I'll call you in and you can program it' " (interview, June 27, 1985).

*Islands of Automation.* Over the years, as information systems developed into a service organization, it began supporting individual organizations within the business: manufacturing, purchasing, accounting, engineering, and so forth. This has occurred not only in the manufacturing industry but in banking, insurance, distribution, health care, and other industries as well. This individualized support eventually caused what I call "islands of automation" to form around organizational boundaries. These islands then solidified the way each organization performed its work. And, once these automated processes were imbedded, it became very difficult to change the way the business was run.

Even within individual functions or departments, old processes—yesterday's functions—are the ones that continue to be automated in an attempt to make them more efficient. However, we have reached a point where there are no productivity gains from this approach. Adding more applications in this manner results in diminishing returns. A company today that is achieving a productivity gain of 1 or 2 percent per year from new computer systems is indeed fortunate. Without considering rising labor or materials costs or any other expenses (which seem to go up every year), we are not getting ahead. We're getting further behind.

And that's the problem. We have reached a point where continuing to automate yesterday's ineffective business practices simply to make them work faster is no longer appropriate. We must look at our business today and how we can use the computer as an enabling technology, a machine that will help us establish new methods of conducting our business. Our scope must encompass the entire business enterprise. Isolated, one-function-at-a-time approaches to automation simply cannot give us the payback we require.

The U.S. steel industry is a prime example of this wrong-headedness. For years, steel firms invested hundreds of millions of dollars in attempts to modernize their old steel mills, trying to remain competitive with overseas steelmakers. They focused on modernizing existing processes, which were designed for the all-purpose, highly integrated mill. Yet these attempts failed. Why? Because they overlooked the fact that integrated mills had become, over the years, very complex and expensive to operate. These firms presumed that the existing processes were satisfactory, and that they simply needed streamlining. However, their Japanese competitors developed minimills, each of which produced just one product. The minimill was a more productive mill and a more profitable one besides.

In another case, our firm became involved with a large manufacturing concern that had decided to take a fresh look at how it was using computer technology. Their goal was to explore major new productivity gains in their business. One area of concentration was automating the shop floor. Everyone was excited at the prospect of using robotics and building a factory of the future.

We began by performing a cost distribution analysis for the entire firm. Of the firm's $1 billion in costs, only $78 million, or 8 percent, was classified as touch labor, or that component of labor costs incurred in the actual process of fabrication, assembly, installation, and inspection of the product—those functions that would be performed by robots. The far more significant costs in other direct and indirect categories—59 percent of total costs—were not even targeted as an area in which technology could improve productivity.

Based on this analysis, the project was redirected to examine and challenge all the existing business practices, including historical organizational alignments. Using computer technology as an enabling device created opportunities to combine functions (such as manufacturing engineering and design engineering) into single entities. Once this was done, the project opened the doors to other innovations in the business processes and created significant productivity breakthroughs.

Rather than merely seeking isolated or incremental opportunities to automate, and obtaining minimal cost reductions, this firm was bold enough to take a hard look at its overall business structure. Once the firm understood the big picture, it developed automation strategies that resulted in productivity gains for the entire company. As a result, the company was able to target cost reductions of 25 to 30 percent.

Changing historical business practices and the company's fundamental organization is not an easy task. It is a change, not only in culture, but in the very nature and process of the work itself. Obviously, various organizations—including information systems—will resist. Yet if the business is going to move away from the existing islands of automation and to reap the benefits of new, advanced computer technology, changes of a more global nature are essential.

*Balancing Technology Planning with Business Planning.* All too often, information systems is developing plans to support its own vision of where the firm is going, while the business planning unit is doing its own planning without considering computer technology implications. Clearly, this must change.

I was working with a major pharmaceutical distribution company several years ago. I suggested that all significant information systems projects, both current and planned, should be reviewed by the firm's senior executives. The executives agreed and in a meeting a few weeks later, a half-completed project with a $600,000 budget came under review.

"Why is information systems working on this project?" the president asked. "We decided to discontinue this method of doing business six months ago." This pointed out the need for continued executive involvement. Once the commitment to these reviews was made, senior management took a more active interest in the information systems department's responsibilities. By the time all the project reviews were completed, the department's application backlog—a matter of considerable concern in most businesses today—was reduced from forty-five thousand staff hours to thirteen-and-a-half thousand staff hours. Because management became more involved in redirecting information systems' energies toward the business, the department felt more active and important to the firm. Together, these two groups began planning projects that benefited the company.

At a large insurance company, a different type of disaster occurred. The firm had entered a new market, trust funds, with a specialized sales force moving aggressively to gain market penetration. After a very successful first year, the company found it did not have the administrative resources to support the trust funds their crack sales force had already sold. The executives decided they needed to automate, but information systems said it would take eighteen months to bring up a new system. The situation grew so severe that the firm discontinued selling activities. By the time they started up again, much of the momentum and focus were lost. A high-growth opportunity had disappeared.

The plain truth is that most information systems planning is not in sync with the business. If technology is going to serve as a tool to help business grow and become more productive, there must be a strong marriage between business planning and information systems planning. Where this occurs, information systems receives clear direction, and a positive relationship develops between the two.

One of the major operations at a major California bank is a good example of this. Information systems, business planners, and the operations executives meet every six months to assure that technology plans are in harmony with the business direction. They meet in all-day sessions. They talk about the business strategy and identify ways technology can help them achieve goals outlined in the strategy. They determine what projects are important. They identify the level of service required to support the business. These meetings create a partnership between information systems and the other organizations.

### How Do We Go Forward?

Your company can begin significant changes right now—today. Not surprisingly, the basic technology tools—hardware, software, and technological know-how—already exist in your information systems department. Your job is to figure out how to set this power free, and deploy it strategically to the firm's advantage.

*Five Criteria for Automation.* Before you leap in and start automating functions, you should ask yourself these five questions:

1. Will we be able to do it cheaper?
2. Will we be able to do it faster?
3. Will we be able to do it better?
4. Will we be able to expand our market?
5. Will it give us a competitive edge?

Once you begin using these five simple questions as your criteria for allocating computer expenditures, your whole perspective will change. These steps do not merely offer a more effective way of evaluating company needs, although they do that, too. Most importantly, they stimulate thought on measurable business goals for the computer function.

Information systems cannot do this by itself, a fact pointed out in a *Wall Street Journal* article. Staff reporter Frank James wrote, "One big problem. Data processing managers, called management information systems (MIS) officers, often treat technology as an end in itself, with little regard for its application."* Information systems managers need to step back a few paces from the technology and gain some perspective. They must understand the firm's mission and how their work relates to it, but they need a business partner who can help them move beyond their concentration on technology to a broader grasp of their role in the business.

*Technology as an Enabling Tool.* Technology should be a tool for business. It should enable business to perform in a more effective manner. We must look at computer technology in new

*Frank James, "Straddling the Spheres." *Wall Street Journal*, Sept. 16, 1985, p. 47c.

ways—ways that will ultimately challenge our historical patterns of thinking. Senior management must take an active, supportive role in putting computer technology to work. This may mean an open advocacy, a culture change, injecting some new ideas and thinking, or a more businesslike approach to using technology.

Information systems as we know it today must become a thing of the past. There must be new missions, new roles, and perhaps a different mix of people. Information systems must become a contribution center rather than a cost center. It must regain its title as the leading-edge organization, the orchestrator and facilitator of change.

The computer is a key instrument in creating and maintaining a competitive position, both in your business and worldwide. There is no single more powerful means for achieving your goals. Both the capability and technology are here. But this is not a simple technology issue. What is really important is how you think about the technology, and how you choose to use it. In his book, *Toward the Next Economics and Other Essays,* Peter F. Drucker wrote:

> Technology is no more mysterious or "unpredictable" than developments in the economy or society. It is capable of rational anticipation and demands rational anticipation. Business managers have to understand the dynamics of technology. At the very least, they have to understand where technological change is likely to have major economic impact and how to convert technological change into economic results.*

*Peter F. Drucker, *Toward the Next Economics and Other Essays* (New York: Harper & Row, 1980), p. 38.

# 2

⊓⊔⊓⊔⊓⊔⊓⊔⊓⊔⊓⊔⊓⊔⊓⊔⊓⊔⊓⊔⊓⊔⊓⊔⊓⊔⊓⊔⊓⊔⊓⊔

# The Identity Crisis
## of Information Systems:
## An Embattled Fortress Under Attack

Today, in more and more U.S. boardrooms, there are heated debates over the quality and quantity of computer services. The undeniable truth is that information systems organizations have a poor image. They do not have the corporation's respect. Their value as an organization, and their ability to work in harmony with others, has come under heavy criticism. Listen to what people are saying:

> We have reached a point where we can no longer expand our business. The computer systems in our company are so structured toward yesterday's business that they are no longer capable of servicing our needs today, let alone our growth requirements.
> —A Chairman of the Board

> What do you consider the greatest block in achieving the long-range business plan? was the question a large corporation's senior management posed to

1

each of its business units. Every manager gave the
same answer: Data processing.
　—From a Company Meeting on Business Objectives

If they would just give us our own mainframe, we
could show MIS how to manage for results.
　　　　　　　　　　　—A User Group Manager

And how does the information systems department respond to
situations like these? One information systems manager said, "I
know what's good for the company. I just put all the requests in
a queue, and sooner or later they go away."

These are just a few of the hundreds upon hundreds of
complaints and comments I have heard over the years. But you
be the judge. How is information systems regarded within your
company? Are your users satisfied with the service they receive?
Is there a touch of frustration in their voices when they talk
about information systems? If not, consider yourself fortunate.

But if you're like the great majority of U.S. businesses,
the battle lines are probably already drawn. Information systems is under attack, both from senior management and user
organizations. There is a siege mentality, and information systems has withdrawn into the walls of a self-created fortress to
protect itself and its turf.

The embattled fortress is the product of a lack of understanding, an absence of shared values, and communication distortion. Information systems, under criticism, had its position
to maintain and its culture to protect; thus the fortress was created. Senior management became frustrated with its inability to
make things change. Information systems, trying to fend off the
criticism, felt more and more like the whipping boy, the organization's John Galt. Even if it wanted to change, its defensive
position made it difficult.

Both sides dug in. Senior management created "emplace-
ments" such as budget cuts and stricter reporting, and also
allowed personal computers that circumvented information systems' authority. Information systems put up its "embattle-

ments": slow maintenance and development, sloppy dress, poor phone etiquette, and so forth.

Why did this occur? Senior management is concerned that what it receives from information systems does not warrant the cost. Users are questioning the value of information systems services. Even information systems management is anxious over the values by which it operates.

To paraphrase the economist Joseph Schumpeter, those things that we value are what contribute to the firm's success. We must find the information systems department's value, and in so doing bring down the walls of the embattled fortress.

## An Identity Crisis

What, exactly, does information systems do? Is it supposed to control the computer and manage the data? Or is it supposed to work closely with the business to identify new computer applications and innovations, possibly leading the way to their use? Why are users obtaining their own computers without the information systems department's approval or cooperation? Why does information systems change its name so often? Over the years a succession of names has been used to identify this function: data processing, computer services, management information systems, and most recently, information resource management. What exactly does "information resource management" mean? Is this an attempt to create an identity?

These questions and many others echo down corporate corridors every day. Information systems lacks a consistent image, inwardly and outwardly. It is often viewed as hypocritical and disingenuous. Information systems management feels abused; they are asked to accomplish ever more assignments while budgets are challenged and new equipment purchases are denied. The staff feels frustrated; as they try to do more and more for the users, they get less and less respect in return.

These and many more examples serve to illustrate the serious nature of the information systems department's identity crisis. Things cannot go on the way they are, for business must have its computers to remain strong and competitive. If we are going to restore its true mission, then we must try to understand the information systems department. As Madame de Staël, the French writer, wrote, "To understand everything makes one tolerant." We may begin by challenging some basic assumptions about computer services.

*Inside the Fortress.* First, let us understand one thing: Information systems is not inherently malevolent, nor is it my purpose here to admonish information systems organizations. As in any field, there is undoubtedly a mix of talented and less-talented individuals.

Information systems is certainly a pawn in a much larger game; many factors have led to the embattled fortress. Consider how the hardware and software makers keep fear of obsolescence at a fever pitch. Executive management's involvement (if it has any at all) has often been adversarial. Users don't understand how to participate usefully or appropriately in new system development. But there are two sides to every question, and information systems must bear its share of responsibility for creating the fortress in which it resides.

We could endlessly debate who is right and who is wrong. What I want to do is challenge us to stop sweeping information systems problems under the rug. The fact is, today's information systems organization is ill-equipped to handle the modern business's computer needs. That is the issue we must deal with— the situation we must correct. Information systems is not going away, and the business cannot do without it.

Many stones have created the fortress walls, set in place by all involved parties. The walls must come down, stone by stone if necessary. Let us consider some of the problems.

• Application development backlog resembles the national debt. Both are huge and neither is under the control of its managers. In some companies, there is a seven-year backlog of user requests caused both by working on things of little value and by an ineffective system of delivering information systems services.

- Maintenance, long considered one of the most important product support services a business provides, is considered a secondary responsibility in information systems. Often it is an afterthought, even though studies indicate that supporting and maintaining important applications in business accounts for fully 50 to 70 percent of the information systems department's budget.

- Computer response time and system availability are inadequate to support the daily requirements of the business. In many companies, terminal response time is estimated not in seconds but in minutes. Consistent, accurate, on-time delivery of computer services is often nonexistent.

- Outdated application programs have become a bane in servicing the business. Most of the applications that business uses today were designed and implemented ten to twenty years ago, supporting yesterday's business needs and practices. It is a tribute to the programmers' skills that they still work as well as they do, but many of these applications have become architecturally unstable and are beginning to impinge on the performance of the business. Using these archaic applications is like trying to make a World War II bomber into a modern jet fighter; neither the bomber nor the applications were designed to support high-performance requirements and the increasingly complex demands of today's world.

- New applications are getting more complex and expensive to implement. A large aerospace firm recently estimated that it would cost $50 million, using traditional programming methods, to redesign its accounting and cost management system. It would then take more than three-and-a-half years to test, debug, and deploy the system. Today's businesses can afford neither such expenditures, nor the time it takes to implement the new application.

- Users have learned a great deal about computers since the early 1980s, and are no longer willing to put up with data processing's recalcitrance and delays. They are acquiring their own computers—micros, minis, and mainframes—and doing their own computing, with or without the information systems department's help.

• Quality, once considered an important attribute in developing any product, is too often lacking in computer-based systems. More often than not, it takes a year or more to iron out the bugs and alleviate the traumas associated with a new system.

• Staff turnover continues to plague information systems organizations. Programmers and analysts skip from shop to shop whenever the whim strikes them. A disagreement with the manager or an unpleasant assignment are enough to send a trained employee across the street. Replacing and retraining key personnel consumes untold millions of dollars every year.

• Information systems resists senior management's involvement, and resents being made accountable for computer systems' performance. Senior management is beginning to question how information systems resources are expended, if the organization is meeting its commitments, and whether or not the level of service is adequate. Information systems, which has never been good at reporting either the good news or the bad, is resisting.

• Within its own organization, information systems management has failed to develop the fundamental business and leadership skills necessary for today's business environment. Senior management, being unable to fully comprehend or appreciate technological accomplishments, is replacing information systems management, in ever greater numbers, from the business side of the house. This is causing even more turmoil and consternation in the information systems rank and file.

I do not believe all these problems can be termed people problems or personality clashes. They are too common and too pervasive throughout industry and government to be lumped into that simple explanation. If we can get beyond the people issues, we may be able to find the real cause, which is *the fundamental manner in which information systems services are dispensed.* In short, perhaps today's information systems methods simply don't work in support of today's—and tomorrow's—business requirements.

Recently, I was working with a company in which both the information systems department and users were so frustrated with each other that they could barely conduct a meeting without antagonism surfacing. When I spoke separately with the users, their solution was quite clear. They wanted to replace the information systems management team and some of the senior staff with competent personnel, or have the computers given to them to manage. Yet when I spoke with the information systems staff, I found they were by and large very capable people. The real causes did not begin to emerge until senior management, the users, and the information systems staff began to meet regularly.

What were these causes? They were the basic structure and design of the applications in use; the tangled, intricate, vulnerable computer network; and the manner of delivering services. These were the blocking factors, not the people. Even more significantly, the company had grown threefold over the past seven years and had undergone significant organizational realignments, yet there was no appreciable change in the way information systems did its work.

At this summit-level meeting, the group addressed each of these issues. Slowly but surely, an entirely new set of principles and structures that defined how information systems services should be delivered in the future began to emerge.

I firmly believe that we, like this group, must step back and question these basic structures that have been in place since the 1960s if we are going to solve today's information systems problems. In so doing, we must not be misled into thinking that some new technology or a faster, bigger computer is the answer. These may contribute to the solution, but the real answer lies in deploying them as tools to change our basic business structure, and as a means for migrating to a more efficient computer services delivery system.

These changes will come neither quickly nor easily. Whenever basic structures are tampered with, resistance forms.

When we have been taught over the years to think or to do things in a particular way, it is difficult to change. But the fact is, unless the information systems department, the users, and senior management challenge the validity of current practices and the underlying cultural premises *together,* then no change will occur.

Real change comes from knowing what you are changing from, and what you are changing to. Let's take a moment to study how today's information systems practices and procedures came into being.

*The Evolution of Computer Architectures.* For all the marketing hype we hear from the computer industry about radical new machines and the latest "artificial intelligence" software, today's computer is, in all its working aspects, the same as its 1940s ancestor. From vacuum tubes to transistors to integrated circuits, all computer designs, or architectures, are based on concepts devised by John von Neumann in 1945.

In the earliest computers, need dictated design. Scientists needed computers capable of solving long, complex equations. Large amounts of data were fed into the machine on punched cards, and with a small amount of luck the computer produced the right answer. This was termed batch processing.

Today, even though we use tapes or disks instead of punched cards, and even though typewriter consoles have been replaced by on-line terminals, the prevailing practices are still the same as they were in the 1950s and 1960s: Many users are hooked up to a large, central computer. Those practices made more sense back then; computers were large and expensive, so it was more cost-effective to have one machine perform many tasks.

But as computers grew smaller and cheaper, our thinking didn't change. Instead of moving computer power out and around the organization, we still saw everything as umbilically tied to the central processor. And, as we tie more devices to the centralized computer, of course we need bigger and bigger processors. Is it that clarion call from the mainframe computer vendors we are hearing again?

This reminds me of the difference between Nikola Tesla and Thomas Edison. Tesla was a genius, perhaps far greater than Edison in many of his achievements. He was able to build a giant electrical coil capable of generating several million volts of electricity. Yet, unlike Edison, Tesla had little interest in harnessing that energy and using it. Once Edison was able to make electricity, his prime interest was how he could wire the world for it.

Information systems is often much like Tesla, mostly interested in computer power for its own sake and far less interested in how it is distributed to the user community. We used to turn to information systems for inspiration and innovation in solving our computer problems, yet they are deeply enmeshed in this centralized thinking.

The fact is, today neither cost nor centralization are critical issues in business computing. With the rise of minicomputers and the proliferation of microcomputers in many different configurations, it's time to begin thinking of computing as an expendable budget item.

We need to rethink many important computer issues. Aren't many of our computer performance problems associated with the complexities inherent in centralized computing? Are we using computers to address the business's real needs and solve its real problems? Are we thinking those problems through carefully to make sure the computer accomplishes the task we want done?

*The Evolution of Computer Applications.* Today's computer applications—the software programs we use to accomplish tasks—had their genesis in the mid- to late-1950s and early 1960s. At the time, two factors determined computer applications design. One, as previously discussed, was the centralized computer concept. Because the machines were so expensive, it made more sense to design and implement programs that automated all or most of the business's major functions and processed them in a single, contiguous pass.

The other factor was personnel: At the time, only a few select people understood the computer's mysteries and how to make it work. Exemplary knowledge and skills were required, for every new application was created from scratch. Niklaus Wirth, a legendary figure in programming, once wrote, "Primarily because of their limitations [the task of programming computers] was achieved by collecting sets of clever techniques and startling tricks."* Indeed, applications became art forms for other programmers to study, and consequently the users' needs and considerations were often set aside in favor of elegant code. In short, applications were designed that forced people to accomplish their work in a way most convenient for the computer, much as if they were on an assembly line.

But the world has changed. Business and government agencies are faced with demands to respond to the marketplace or to social pressures more quickly and more effectively. Control and flexibility are far more important attributes in doing one's job today. There are ever more demands for improvements and enhancements in existing business processes.

However we structure future applications, we must recognize that the need for flexibility is always going to be with us. Continuing to design enormously complex computer application programs does little to support the modern business environment.

## The Information Systems Profession

Information systems is one of the most diverse and eclectic professions in business. Most information systems people are self-taught, having come from anthropology, finance, music, mathematics, physics, and a variety of other disciplines. In fact, there was no formal degree program in computer science until the mid-1960s.

There is no such thing as a typical "computer person" and most seem to pride themselves on that fact. More often than not they think of themselves as creative types, as seen in their dress, diet, irregular hours, and loner attitude. As a result,

*Niklaus Wirth, "On the Composition of Well-Structured Programs," in *Classics in Software Engineering* (New York: Yourdon Press, 1974), p. 153.

they often regard themselves as different from other employees, somehow outside the normal rules and conventions that govern the business. This, needless to say, has created resentment and frustration throughout the firm.

But the high priesthood of information systems has come to an end. Today, thousands of managers and users know as much about how computers should be used as do the information systems personnel—at least enough to accomplish their own work, using the computer unaided.

Information systems began the transformation from a creative think tank to a professional organization in the mid-1970s, establishing structure, work procedures, and, of course, its bureaucracies. Unfortunately, it was at the pinnacle of the large computer era when centralized computing, batch processing, and company-wide systems prevailed. The information systems department's culture was built on the first twenty-five years of computer technology concepts, and therein lies the crux of the problem: organizational structures, controls, and methods of operation were based on knowledge and experiences that had matured and were about to be retired.

The world was moving on, and information systems was prepared neither for the new wave of technological innovation nor for the revolution in business practices just beginning. In many information systems organizations I have worked with in recent years I see organizational structures, responsibilities, and thinking that are identical to those in organizations I managed in the 1950s and 1960s. Information systems, the organization with access to state-of-the-art technology, continues to hang on to theories and concepts from the Industrial Age. What's worse, they are taking tomorrow's technology and forcing it to conform to yesterday's information systems practices and concepts.

Yet while we scold information systems for its lack of insight and professionalism, senior management on the other hand has not created a sufficient climate for change. Information systems has rarely been asked, What are your criteria for implementing computer systems in our company? or told, Here is how we expect the new computer system to benefit the organization in time, money, and productivity gains. Information systems has not been told, You have enough computers. Now let's see how they can help us become more profitable and productive.

There is a rift in values and expectations here that subsequently created a communication distortion, leading to the embattled fortress we have today. The problem has become serious —so serious that small changes can no longer make a difference. It took both senior management and information systems to build the fortress walls, and it will take drastic measures to bring those walls down.

## The Quest

Some of those changes may be painful or difficult for everyone concerned, yet none are terminal in nature. Many managers want to avoid disputes and problems, hoping the problem will either go away or, at best, will not grow more acute before they retire. Yet there is no way to ignore or abdicate responsibility. This problem affects the entire corporation.

Creating the future must be done in concert with people from outside the information systems organization. The computer must become a resource and a productivity tool for everyone in the firm. First, we must ask, What is the information systems organization's charter? If one does not exist, it is certainly time to create one. We must then ask, What is its role in the organization? I believe the role is achieving productivity gains and increasing efficiency; as I have asked before, will we be able to do it better, faster, or cheaper? Further, is it expanding our market or enhancing the competitive advantage for the business?

The quest is to find the best of both the old and the new that the computer offers, without making life more complicated with all this talk about "information management" or "information resources." The information systems organization must be revitalized and must shoulder its role as the prime mover in the firm's progress and success, while at the same time continuing to support daily needs. In short, we need clear and simple goals that will help information systems regain its stature as the firm's leading-edge organization.

To this end, I believe it would be helpful to give information systems a name that reflects its true mission. If we go back in time far enough, we find that companies used to have a *computer technology department.* (This, I might add, was after they outgrew "The IBM Room.") Because our mission is the harmonious merging of business and technology goals, I propose we rename information systems the *business technology department.* It is a return to basics, to simplicity. Where there is simplicity there is clarity of purpose, function, and mission. Further, I believe the department should deliver what its name implies: essential technology that supports all aspects of the business enterprise.

The business technology department (or just *business technology*), as I will refer to it in the ensuing chapters, is the company's nerve center, supplying energy and stimulation to all who require it. Your quest is to assure that the computer, and the business technology department, fulfill this promise. As the quester, it is your task to affect this change. Your success ensures that the company will succeed and prosper in the years ahead.

# 3

꩜꩜꩜꩜꩜꩜꩜꩜꩜꩜꩜꩜꩜꩜꩜꩜꩜꩜꩜꩜꩜꩜

# Myths, Assumptions, and Realities
About Business Technology

I have suggested that, in order to succeed at our quest of transforming the business technology department into a productive
organization within the firm, we must begin by giving a great
deal of thought to the problem. Where do we begin? First, by
stepping back and saying: There must be a better way. A proactive stance is essential; we must be convinced that change is
required and success is possible.

Most U.S. businesses are no longer conducting business
the way they were in the 1960s and 1970s. Our management
techniques have also changed. Systems and procedures that
made sense then simply aren't appropriate today. Now is the
time to look for a new framework—a new system architecture—
that will support our needs both today and into the future. To
do so, we need the support and the services of business technology—that organization we previously referred to as information
systems. But first, we must rid ourselves of old, unacceptable
notions about computers and prepare to embrace new concepts
and techniques.

There are numerous myths to dispel. Many myths have
sprung up from business technology's history, creating legends

and folklore that many accept today as truth. Hardware and software companies continue to propagate these myths (which are based on yesterday's thinking) because they help sell more products. The latest piece of hardware or most recent version of an application program may temporarily improve the situation, but in most cases it only begins to address future needs. Hardware and software cannot answer the problems until we dispel the myths. Here are some of the myths that are trotted out as truths in business technology.

### The Myth That Computing Power Must Be Centralized

If you remember automobiles in the 1960s, you probably recall they had powerful motors and were quite large. The prevailing mentality could be characterized as "bigger is better."

Many who began working with computers during this period saw the IBM System/360—so named because there are 360 degrees in a perfect circle, hence the perfect computer system—become the most popular computer in the world. Most business people thought of the computer as a utility, like an electrical generator or the heating and cooling system, so it was natural to centralize its functions.

This was fine when computers were large and expensive. However, it's a sheer myth that we need to keep computers inside the glass-walled room. As I've suggested before, today's business procedures are physically organized where they do the most good. The same should be true with computers: Put them where they are used. Anything else is simply a case of perpetuating old thinking, and that is what needs to be changed.

### The Myth That a Bigger Processor Is Better

As it has grown larger, the computer system has grown increasingly more complex to manage and operate. The operating systems have been pushed to the highest level of generalization, so they can manage hundreds of programs concurrently. At any given moment, the central processor may be simultaneously operating on a mathematical model, the payroll, on-line order

entry, inventory control, shop floor scheduling, on-line cash
management, and information center processing.

The level of complexity is so high that it's often unman-
ageable. In large computer complexes, you will find application
jobs being passed from processor to processor, seeking either
available time or the appropriate data base for processing. In
some computer centers, a transaction may have to move through
twenty different hardware units before it can be processed,
often tying up the system needlessly. If any one unit fails, the
system becomes inoperative for that transaction. The end result
is that users perceive the computer to be down, or out of order.

## The Myth That Good Computer Systems
## Must Be Complex

Business technology people often like to point out the
technological complexities of the computer system they work
on, as if that made their computer better. The price they pay
for this complexity can be very high, for three things are likely
to occur. First, the probability of failure increases. Second, the
failures are more likely to be serious. Third, it is far more difficult to locate problems and failures when they occur. In a word,
we have reached a level of complexity that borders on the un-
manageable.

Computer systems need not be complex. Usually, what
makes them so are the various features and functions required
for the users. This "user functionality" is a two-edged sword. It
is where the greatest amount of innovation occurs, but it is also
where the most programming maintenance is required.

It doesn't make sense to burden the central processor
with this much unnecessary complexity. It works against our
goal to provide simple, trouble-free computing services for the
organization. If we isolate some of these functions and move
them away from the central computer, out to where the user
needs them and can use them more freely and creatively, we
have achieved two goals. We have simplified the interface and
untangled some of the rat's nest we have in today's centralized
complexes. And we have made the system easier and less expensive to maintain.

### The Myth That Computer Power Is Increasing
### While Cost Is Decreasing

A popular assumption about the promise of computers is that the power is increasing while the cost is steadily decreasing. But the paradox is that though the cost of computers has declined, the cost of computer centers has doubled or tripled over the same period. Why? A major factor is the highly complex computer systems we just discussed. Operating system software must be more sophisticated, and requires many more computer cycles to manage the computer system. The large number of application programs running at a given time requires larger memories and more computer cycles, too. And, of course, tuning and balancing a more complex computer system requires more staff.

Yet even with a highly trained staff doing performance monitoring, systems tuning, and capacity planning, the computer still grows so overburdened that performance deteriorates below acceptable levels, or the computer is constantly "crashing." It reminds me of my days in the aerospace industry. A rocket engine was designed, say, for five hundred thousand pounds of thrust. The engineers would tweak it, fine-tune it, and modify it to get a little more performance, but finally, and inevitably, it would blow up. All machines can reach a point of structural instability. When this occurs, it is time to employ new concepts and new structures. It is time to move on to the next technological level.

### The Myth of the Giant, All-Encompassing Data Base

The need for a corporate data base management system, or DBMS, is fundamental to the argument for integrated, centralized applications. This myth presumes that one giant data base should be the repository for all the company's data, and that everyone in the company should have equal access to the data. This idea stems from the new theory that information is a resource, the same as people or capital. If, the theory continues, you believe that the "information" stored in your data base is of equal value to capital, then why aren't you profiting from it?

There are two things wrong with this myth. First, the fact is that only a small percentage of the data—and that's all it is, pure and simple data—stored in the central data base has any value other than at the particular point in time that it's stored. It might be the day's cash reserves, a memorandum, or an update to an employee file. Its usefulness usually stops there. Second, if we were to analyze the data that has more than one-time value, we would find that less than 20 percent of it needs to be shared outside the originating organization. Yet we spend millions of dollars buying more and more centralized mass storage devices for the data base, on the off chance that somebody may need something, some time.

We should not be interested in building monumental data bases. Why not break the data base down into manageable units that serve individual organizations? Let purchasing have their own data base. Let accounting, quality assurance, logistics, materiel, and production control have their own. Whatever small amounts of data that need to be shared can be duplicated by the originating organization, as required, in the central data base.

Moreover, if we made data bases a little smaller, we could have quicker access to them. We'd use the data to solve problems more easily. Best of all, we'd reduce system complexity dramatically.

There is a great deal of interest today in using relational data base management systems and fourth-generation languages to solve our large data base problems. I strongly advocate their use, but not to sustain large, centralized data bases. We need to rethink the underlying reasons for a centralized data base and how we use the data before we begin employing new, and often expensive, technologies.

### The Myth That Controlling Business Technology Requires Taking a Hard Line on Costs

Taking a hard line on costs may be appropriate to achieve an immediate profit goal of the business. However, when this hard line is used to control the performance of business technology, as it often is, it doesn't work.

First of all, computers and their supporting organization, business technology, have become a vital arm in the delivery performance of business. Cutting their cost without reducing their objectives will only further dilute their performance, and will ultimately create inefficiency within other organizations in the business. Further, in almost every instance, as there is a decline in computing services there is a rise in computer and system purchases outside the business technology organization. Therefore, no containment of costs is achieved; costs are just shifted to another place, and for the wrong reason as well.

Any notions of establishing a hard line on business technology costs should be considered carefully. That does not mean business shouldn't expect a fair return on its business technology dollars, or that a shake-up to get rid of nonproductive overhead isn't a good idea from time to time. What it does mean is that if you are dissatisfied with the value received from your business technology expenditures, don't expect that controlling cost is the answer. You need to identify and attack the real problem, whatever that might be in your particular situation.

### The Myth of the Incompetent User

Business technology often feels it must protect the user from the internal goings-on related to the computer room. I disagree. Over the past few years, I have seen the most brilliant conceptual thinking about computer systems come from the users. They have a clear vision of how to exploit technology to their own advantage and thus achieve the company's missions and goals. Users are becoming the technological innovators, as well as the visionaries for future system design concepts.

Much of this can be credited to the personal computer revolution of the 1980s, for this machine truly brought computing out of the glass-walled room. When business technology said a task or application was not possible, the user replied, But I can do it on my personal computer. Why can't you do it on your mainframe? Often business technology replied, Well, you must be doing something wrong, or, That's not the kind of thing you're supposed to do with your computer.

These are purely defensive reactions, and this is where business technology let everyone down. When that became apparent, it's no wonder users looked for their own solutions. Clearly users, in their own way, can be every bit as knowledgeable as the computer staff. But it's time to begin developing some mutual trust and respect between the business technology organization and user organizations. I would like to see them working together to create the future.

## The Myth That Business Technology People Are a Special Breed

The business technology department cites many reasons for its problems, and they all share one thing in common: They are excuses. Overworked, understaffed, harassed, underbudgeted —none of these excuses have anything to do with the real problem. Gerald M. Weinberg describes perhaps the greatest apology for the business technology department in his book, *The Psychology of Computer Programming*:

> If asked, most programmers would probably say they preferred to work alone in a place where they wouldn't be disturbed by other people. . . . There is no doubt that the majority of people in programming today lean in the "detached" direction, both by personal choice and because hiring policies for programmers are often directed toward finding such people. And, to a great extent, this is a good choice, because a great deal of programming work is "alone and creative."*

This is not only misleading, it's also the crux of business technology's problem: the self-fulfilling prophecy. The reclusive, introverted, I-want-to-be-alone image is often thought of as the natural order of computer people. The fact is, there are no more

*Gerald M. Weinberg, *The Psychology of Computer Programming* (New York: Van Nostrand Reinhold, 1971), pp. 52–53.

introverts, loners, or misfits in computing than there are in any other profession. Most business people, whether presidents, middle managers, or mailroom clerks, would prefer more peace and quiet and fewer interruptions in their work. What makes business technology people think they're so special?

I have mentioned that many people came to business technology from other fields. Most of them sought more excitement, structure, and consistency in their work. A logical machine like the computer and methodical work like programming appealed to them. Yet all too often they did not find the consistent practices and procedures they desired. Business technology, which should have been methodical and orderly, was in truth quite chaotic. It wasn't a very professional environment. Newcomers either succumbed to the general disorganization or left for another line of work.

That's the self-fulfilling prophecy: People in business technology think, because there is no structure, I don't have to follow any set procedures. Without structure, standards, and procedures, I can do my own thing. That makes me, in Weinberg's words, one of those "alone and creative" people.

This certainly does not contribute to a spirit of professionalism. What it leads to, in fact, is a department full of nonresponsive prima donnas. To me, it's one big rationalization. I prefer the more constructive kind of self-fulfilling prophecy: If we stop making excuses and adopt a professional attitude, we'll all become professionals. Every field, from accounting to engineering to auto mechanics, has the ability to project a professional image. Business technology is no exception. Stop giving the business technology staff excuses to think they are a special breed.

### The Myth That Restructuring Business Technology Means All the Programmers Will Leave

This is a cry that my principals and I hear quite often when we recommend an organizational change. The plain fact is, the programmers don't leave. We must first ask the question, What needs to be done? Change is inevitable, but not neces-

sarily for the worse. There will always be a variety of assignments and opportunities available. The people who choose to
leave may be the ones you wouldn't miss anyway.

Although our goal is to disperse computer services, there
will always be a central facility, and it needs to be maintained.
In many cases, programmers and analysts will work in user organizations. Why are we so worried that they may not accept
the change? In many, many cases they are happier with their
new-found involvement. Moreover, if you analyze the business
technology department's staff assignments, you may find a
number of programmers and analysts who are, for all intents
and purposes, already working on an everyday basis with the
users. There may not be any change other than reporting relationships.

In any event, business technology should feel cause to
rejoice, for the great burden of providing computing services
for the entire company has been lifted from its shoulders. Eventually, this will cause business technology to be set free from its
enormous application backlog. Now the less-demanding projects
can be developed by users, while the business technology is
able to concentrate on other more sophisticated applications.

I have discussed only a few of the pervasive myths about
business technology. As you begin solving your firm's computer
problems, you will likely encounter many more. Each must be
addressed and dealt with. You cannot develop tomorrow's
architecture unless you fully understand today's roadblocks.
Keep your mind open; listen carefully; respond candidly. Challenge the myths, break them down, and dispel them.

Users will assuredly welcome these changes, but business
technology must embrace them as well. It must reevaluate its
long-standing opinion that people who understand computers
must be controlled through a central organization. The computer cannot—must not—stay in the back room. Business technology must expand its horizons from being simply a computer
services organization to one that also provides education, consulting, and leadership so that users can grow and become more
productive.

# 4

꒒꒒꒒꒒꒒꒒꒒꒒꒒꒒꒒꒒꒒꒒꒒꒒꒒꒒꒒꒒꒒꒒꒒꒒꒒꒒꒒꒒꒒꒒

# The Enlightened Breed
of Computer Users:
Agents of Innovation
in the Business

The debut of the microcomputer, or personal computer as it is commonly referred to, is another issue we must contend with. It has changed the world of computers dramatically. Suddenly, overnight, computing power was inexpensive and accessible. What's more, it was easy to learn to use the PC and its software. In a very short time, the business world had coined a term for white-collar workers using PCs: *the knowledge user.* Knowledge users and PCs have brought about a renaissance in the office, creating what I term *the era of the enlightened user.*

The PC is an amazing machine; it graduated from amateur to professional status in just a few years. Serious business computing became a reality in 1979, when Dan Bricklin and Bob Frankston introduced VisiCalc, the world's first electronic spreadsheet. Wave upon wave of applications software flooded the market thereafter: word processors, data base managers, in short, every kind of software that previously ran on mainframe machines, and a few new ones besides. But microcomputer software was a little different. Software designers knew their products were for novices, and created their products accordingly.

The business and trade press were quick to pick up on the trend. In no time, there were columns or sections on personal computing in every major magazine and newspaper. The hardware and software makers quickly became an industry that had its own press corps, which provided coverage that was way out of proportion with the industry's 10-percent share of the gross national product.

The newsstands were soon awash with over three hundred specialized computing magazines. They all shared one thing in common: Never print a discouraging word. In 1982, *Time* magazine appointed the PC its Man of the Year. *The New York Times* launched a twice-weekly personal computing column. *The Wall Street Journal, Fortune, Business Week,* and others gave reporters the Silicon Valley as their exclusive beat. Every major business and science magazine had a computer section.

New York publishing houses were suddenly in a frenzy to publish books on computers. There was no subject too mundane or too esoteric, from learning to use a popular word processor to exploring disk maintenance and backup techniques to artificial intelligence. Bookstores overflowed with computer books. Many established separate sections filled with hundreds of titles that less than 5 percent of the population could understand.

Learning to use a personal computer was universally acknowledged as a virtue, regardless of how easy, difficult, or appropriate it was supposed to be. Although that irrepressible fervor has subsided, "micromania" still remains one of the most subtle and persistent promotional campaigns in history. And yet it took away the stigma of keyboard contact, transforming computers from outré to chic. Once the notion of personal productivity became popular, there was no stopping the trend. Getting a PC was as easy as getting a typewriter.

## Personal Computing Versus Corporate Computing

People like to control their own resources, and that's exactly what the PC gave them. They could use the computer whenever they wanted. They could design, create, and format their own reports. They were in charge; they felt more productive and better able to make a significant contribution to the firm. It is interesting to note that Adam Smith was aware of this phenomenon:

> Every individual necessarily labors to render the annual revenue of the society as great as he can. . . . He intends only his own gain, and he is in this, as in many other cases, led by an invisible hand to promote an end which was no part of his intention. . . . By pursuing his own interest he frequently promotes that of the society more effectually than when he really intends to promote it.*

Unfortunately, as soon as PCs began to proliferate, business technology management sought ways to control them—controlling them based on the old ways of thinking, and controlling them the wrong way.

Business technology restricted access to corporate mainframe data. They gave higher priority to mainframe reports than to PC-generated reports. They controlled and managed PCs through information centers. A vice president at a large East Coast bank told me their information center was established "to control PC proliferation," as if it were a disease or a bug infestation.

## Too Little Versus Too Much

Fortunately, the personal computer issue has become more balanced since the early days. Business technology no longer tries to control every aspect of personal computing, and users no longer believe the PC is a panacea.

And though there are problems with the mainframe computer, there are problems with PCs as well. PCs were supposed

---

*Adam Smith, *An Inquiry into the Nature and Causes of the Wealth of Nations* (New York: Britannica Great Books, 1952; originally published in 1776), p. 193.

to increase personal productivity, yet often productivity declined during the learning curve. Much of the time users spent learning the machine and its software was time they should have spent attending to business, a revenue loss impossible to estimate.

Or consider the fact that as many users gained proficiency with the PC, their desire to master every other aspect of computing grew accordingly. They began writing their own programs, often when a company-approved, off-the-shelf program would do. Often they replicated an application that ran on the mainframe. This lack of standards led to problems in sharing data with co-workers, and cost the company in dollars as well as in lost productivity.

Before long, PC users wanted to connect their computers to the mainframe so they could withdraw corporate data for use in their application programs. Often they wanted to send updated data back to the mainframe, too. There were no standards for this procedure or for maintaining the data's integrity, so the personal computer created a whole new set of service headaches.

Knowledge users found it was neither possible nor feasible to perform on their PCs every task a mainframe computer could do. Senior management and knowledge users alike found that not everyone needed to learn about computers; in fact, they found that some people should *not* learn to use them. Senior management learned it must pay strict attention to the difference between need and fascination.

### The Importance of Knowledge Users

The PC peppered the firm with people who understood the computer—knowledge users. Knowledge users have made three important contributions to the modern office. First, they have proven it is possible to use the PC to solve a wide variety of business problems. Before PCs, most offices in this country used tools and techniques that had been in place for over a hundred years. Reports weren't revised because they took too long to retype. Financial projections weren't updated because recalculating was arduous. Lacking many of the computer's analytical tools, seat-of-the-pants decisions were common.

Second, knowledge users have proven that average people can easily learn to operate the computer. Often, knowledge users don't even realize how well they understand the computer. They do things the business technology department thought could not be done.

Third, today's knowledge users may become tomorrow's enlightened users. Their experience is helping them understand the dynamics between business functions and computer functions. As many knowledge users learn from their experiences and assume greater responsibilities in the company, they will spearhead tomorrow's innovations.

Yet with all these changes occurring, the business technology department seems unable to grasp what is happening all around it. They see machines and are aware of data moving, but they don't see the implications. And they're still clinging to the old ways of doing things.

The knowledge user clearly has exceeded the business technology department's limits of imagination, has created new uses and applications, and has transformed computer systems. This is laudable. This is what was supposed to happen in the evolution of computers that was arrested in the mid-1970s. But often that attitude is a bit simplistic as well, because it's still true that some applications are more difficult to implement on a large, complex organizational computer than on a smaller desktop PC.

And it is here that we must be careful: The purpose of giving knowledge users PCs is not simply so they can learn how a computer works, as I mentioned earlier. It is so they may gain an understanding of the technology and use it to solve business problems.

But how do we harness this shift in energy and innovation without repeating the old information systems patterns of control? This is the challenge: to find a way to balance innovation against application. We must allow the education process to continue without becoming mired in technology for technology's sake. We cannot afford to make the same mistakes again.

## The Emerging Enlightened User

There is a new breed of leader emerging from the tension between business technology and knowledge users. Magazine articles, books, and advertisements have encouraged a tremendous amount of education on computers, data processing, and information management. People are concerned about the continued escalation of business technology costs without corresponding benefits. These and other factors have had a profound effect on those who are unwilling to accept the business technology status quo any longer.

These people have assessed the disputes and asked, What's there to fight about? They have looked at the business and at the computer, and they have determined there is something of value here. They have looked at the way things are done and have concluded that change must occur if the firm is going to get value from the computer. They have a new perspective. They are the enlightened users.

The enlightened user understands that computer technology is the vehicle for creating change. The technology can change business patterns; it enables the firm to produce its products and services more competitively. You cannot change people, nor can you change business patterns, unless people will accept a motivating force. That force is computer technology.

Brian Boyer, vice-president of central manufacturing for Northrop Aircraft, put it this way:

> There is little question in my mind that a company can by sheer power reduce costs by 20 percent. The problem is that if power is used, it won't stay. Whatever is done, the costs will always creep back in. They cannot keep the pressure on that long. Technology will force a change in the process of how we do business. It will provide a new baseline. It will cause a permanent change. Sheer power is replaced by new business practices. When you change the manner in which you build your product, you can build it with less people in less time.

> Using the computer as an enabling technology al-
> lows you to change the basic processes. Then
> comes the *real* change [consulting engagement,
> May 1985].

Henry Ford did this when he used the assembly line to build autos. He reduced the number of people, thereby reducing the cost of production. Because his autos were less expensive, the demand for them doubled. Ford changed the way he did business and became more productive at the same time.

Brian Boyer is an enlightened user. He says he's tired of hearing "I can't" from the business technology department, as well as from users, and is solving his particular problems by questioning the entire process:

> Can we gain productivity by looking at the process
> in a new way? Can we gain productivity by com-
> bining functions, such as engineering and manu-
> facturing engineering? What if we could put rou-
> tines in a computer so that when the product is
> designed, tests could automatically be made to see
> if that design could be manufactured. If that is pos-
> sible, then we could conceivably cut in half the
> lead time to build the product, reduce labor costs,
> and produce the product for less. And if our prod-
> ucts cost less, demand for them could increase
> [consulting engagement, May 1985].

This kind of strategic thinking about ways to maximize the utility of the business technology department can be applied to banking, insurance, distribution, or government agencies—in fact, to any area of commerce. Enlightened users like Brian Boyer are always at work, thinking of new ways to get the most from the computer resource. They have made significant contributions to the way we apply computers in business. Not only do they have a keen business sense, but they truly understand and appreciate the fact that the computer can make business more productive. What's more, they know how to make it happen.

The enlightened user does not have a profound technical knowledge of the computer, but also does not fear or misapprehend its purpose. This user knows what is possible and what is not, and recognizes the difference between a useful application and a poor or inappropriate one. Enlightened users are unique people who understand both the firm's business needs and goals, and computer technology. They are the firm's unwitting key innovators. They are on the leading edge of tomorrow's organization. They probably don't understand the impact they have, nor do they understand where it's all going yet. But nevertheless, they have launched a shift in the firm's creative energies; they have formed a two-way flow with business technology where once it was just one-way. They are attempting to forge new links between user organizations and business technology, rather than creating more divisions. They are creating tomorrow's stronger, more productive business environment by dispelling the old myths and demolishing the embattled fortress.

The enlightened users are largely responsible for assuring that the computer is a useful and productive tool for the firm. They have evoked a profound change in how others view the computer resource. Enlightened users realize that the computer is the primary vehicle for changing and improving the way we do business. It enables us to produce a better or less-expensive product, or to get the product out more efficiently.

### Enlightened Users: A Profile

Enlightened users come from many walks of life, but all share several things in common. First, they are able to see the relationship between the computer and the firm's business goals. Second, they are conceptual thinkers, and are able to figure out how a computer application could effectively automate the business function in question.

Some enlightened users come from the business side of the firm, yet understand the technical side of computers well enough to see their use in solving business problems. They may never have used a computer personally, but that is unimportant. What is important is knowing when one is needed and how it can get the job done. They have a sense and a feel for the computer and its work, and understand almost intuitively when it could improve a business function.

Other enlightened users come from a technical background, but have learned the business side of the enterprise. They too are conceptual people, and are able to create innovative computer applications that are, above all else, useful and appropriate for the business function. They see the computer as a tool for solving business problems.

Whether they come from the business side or the technical side, enlightened users are creating a new synergy between the two. They want to see the computer perform for the good of the company.

In my experience, enlightened users are most visible in the top ranks of the firm. They are often members of senior management who have grown deeply frustrated, and are no longer willing to wait for change to occur. They have thought a great deal about the problems and have developed insight and perspective. They believe they know the solution, and know what they want to do.

Other enlightened users are emerging below the senior management ranks as well. In fact, they are emerging in all areas of the corporation, and are making their presence felt. William G. McGowan, chairman of MCI Communications Corporation, says, "Individuals who possess *both* business and information technology skills could become invaluable to their companies, and highly prized candidates in the job market" (personal communication, March 1987).

## Catalysts Today and Tomorrow

I recall when engineers began changing from analog to digital equipment. The entire conversion process took fifteen years. The enlightened user phenomenon is just beginning. It will be years before enough enlightened users emerge to demand all the needed changes. There is much yet to discover. For now, the most important thing is to understand the phenomenon, then work to move it ahead.

The PC has been a powerful catalyst in business. It gave us enlightened users, knowledge users, and new hope for enhancing productivity with computers. We have seen innovative new software such as relational data base managers, spreadsheets, and artificial-intelligence-inspired decision support systems. The PC has hastened the development of English-like natural languages and fourth-generation languages, replacing awkward and difficult-to-learn programming languages. Clearly, catalysts abound because there is a synergy between the business users and the software developers.

Tomorrow's enlightened user must keep this synergy alive and at the same time find more catalysts. Equally important, tomorrow's catalysts must not be a reaction against the business technology department, as they often are today. Both enlightened users and the business technology department are important, integral aspects of the firm, and they must coexist for the firm to reach its goals.

The enlightened user must exemplify this harmony throughout the company. He or she must be a business innovator and a systems manager at the same time, blending the two together to achieve business goals. The truly enlightened user is on a quest seeking the proper information that brings results. To them, the computer is simply a means to an end, as it was originally intended.

### Vision and Renewal

Vision is essential to effecting change. This concept is well known. It means that senior management and the enlightened user must think, reflect, discuss, and plan ways to make the most of the various computer resources. For example, you must help knowledge users find a balance between freedom and control. They must be guided and trained to make technological decisions that are in the company's best interests. Invite them to meetings that include enlightened users, business technology managers, and senior management. Create focus groups and roundtable discussions to solve problems and develop strategies.

The business technology department often fears that

once outsiders step in, whether they are enlightened users or senior management, users will be taught methods and techniques that are inconsistent with their own. They are right, but for the wrong reasons. Users have learned about computers on their own, and genuinely see better ways to get the work accomplished. The business technology people must constantly be challenged; remember, they learned their ways in the 1950s, 1960s, or 1970s. The purpose is to use computers in the most efficient way possible.

Renewal is just as important as vision. Business technology must not be a loser but a partner. Whatever strategies and plans are employed, remember that the mistakes business technology made must not be passed on to the new generation of users. Business technology is a coequal keeper of the new computer technology. If sound methodologies and procedures had been in place early on, users would already be in partnership with the business technology department.

Even in saying this, I realize it is often difficult to decide where to begin changing an infrastructure so diffuse and multifaceted as the one created by computers. But remember, it was created by people, not machines. People can change it again. Enlightened users, by their very nature, seek this kind of order and efficiency. They are able to transcend the parochial views of various factions—user departments, the business technology department, even senior management—and move the quest forward.

But remember, this is uncharted country. These changes are profound, and must be carefully nourished and cultivated. As I mentioned, it took enlightened engineers fifteen years to convert the world from analog to digital computers. This new task will take time, too. But now there is a whole new force that never existed before, one that is changing the complexion of what business technology can and will be. That force is the enlightened user. Innovation cannot—must not—be the sole purview of business technology. Enlightened users will push for entirely different ways to manage and implement computer technology. That is the quest.

*PART TWO*

---

# Restoring the Promise
# of Information Systems

The use of technology in the future can either be controlled by us, or it will occur haphazardly. If people using computers are allowed to go their own ways, individual systems will not be integrated into the business; anarchy is the ultimate result. In order for technology to benefit our business and allow us to achieve productivity and our competitive goals, we must be looking ahead and developing future strategies. Tomorrow's business computer systems architecture must integrate the business's needs with the technology's potential, offering us the opportunity to use the ultimate powers of the computer as a business tool. Chapters Five through Seven offer ideas and strategies for how to do this.

# 5

⊓⎍⊓⎍⊓⎍⊓⎍⊓⎍⊓⎍⊓⎍⊓⎍⊓⎍⊓⎍⊓⎍⊓⎍⊓⎍⊓⎍⊓⎍⊓⎍⊓⎍⊓⎍⊓⎍⊓⎍

# Tearing Down the Fortress Walls: Dispersing Computer Power

We have experienced tremendous changes in recent decades, but none so swift or so dramatic as those involving computers. Since the mid-1940s, we have compressed the power of a machine standing two stories high, weighing forty tons, and filling a gymnasium into a slice of silicon the size of your little fingernail. Just fifteen years ago, there were only two kinds of computers: the mainframe, the more compact descendent of UNIVAC; and the minicomputer, brainchild of Kenneth Olsen, who founded Digital Equipment Corporation. Even the minicomputer wasn't small; one might not fill a room, but it could certainly have dominated it.

Today, we not only have mainframes, but everything from supercomputer mainframes to small-system mainframes to desktop superminis to briefcase microcomputers.

With all these choices, there should be no reason why we cannot get the right computing power, along with the right application software, into the users' hands. But in fact, the existing centralized computing scheme does not permit it. It does not support today's ways of getting work done. I am convinced that *dispersing computer technology* is the way to restore the lost promise of computer productivity to U.S. business.

To illustrate my point, consider what happened when the business technology department for a large county in a Midwestern state tried to maintain its centralized hegemony. This organization used an IBM 3081 for conventional off-line batch processing, such as payroll, welfare, voter registration, and the like, which was perfectly acceptable. However, the county hospital needed a system for twenty-four-hour-a-day, on-line, real-time computer services. Patient records had to be updated immediately; doctors needed status reports at all times of the day and night; administrative records had to be kept current on a day-to-day basis.

The county's business technology manager wanted to keep all the computer power centralized, so he said his people could handle the hospital on their IBM 3081. This seemed practical and cost-effective, so it was approved.

Business technology was able to get the hospital on the system all right, but trying to run both a batch processing system and a real-time system on the same computer proved to be a bad idea. The hospital response time was more than two minutes—enough time to cost a patient his or her life. Furthermore, system performance for the county offices was reduced, too. No users were getting the service they deserved.

The problem was in the attempt to support vastly different processing requirements—two entirely different business missions—on one computer. When my company was called in, we recommended separating the two systems and giving the hospital its own computer. The business technology manager didn't like it, for he'd lost some control—and some face. But this old-fashioned way of looking at computer usage represents a kind of wrongheadedness that we simply cannot afford any longer. As the case of this county department illustrates, the cost is too great—in money, in lost productivity, and in lost opportunity.

### Dispersed Computing

Whether it's putting a mainframe computer like the IBM 3081 in the hospital or a desktop microcomputer in front of the CFO for cash management, I call putting computer power

where it is needed *dispersed computing*. Envision a large corporation—perhaps your own—with many separate computers in
various departments or offices, all getting work done, all con-
tributing to the firm's productivity. There may be terminals
connected to the mainframe, some minicomputer systems, or
workstation clusters. There may also be numerous stand-alone
machines, such as desktop microcomputers or individual workstations. The centralized mainframe computer still plays an
important role; it performs tasks that influence a variety of
functions and organizations in the company. However, many
organizations, functions, and groups are free to do their own
computing, using their own computers.

There is no centralized responsibility as we know it today
for all these computers; much of the computer power is under
the direct supervision of the users themselves or the user organization management. This is dispersed computing. It may seem
at first that there is no order to the plan, but I assure you a
carefully thought out architecture guides the dispersal, which I
will explain in more detail in Chapter Six.

## How Dispersed Computing Is Different

At first, you may think this is simply another variation
on old architectural ideas (such as decentralized or distributed
computing) that have already been played out. This is not the
case.

*Decentralized Computing.* Decentralized computing, by
its very name, would appear to be the antithesis of centralized
computing. However, decentralized only means breaking apart
and scattering management responsibility for the computing
function. It is meant to imply, Here is your computer, now go it
alone. But the scattered organization ends up being structured
in the same manner as the centralized organization it was
spawned from, causing services to be dispensed in the same way.
The result is many smaller, centralized locations. There has been
no change in the delivery process to the user because the control concepts have not changed.

To my mind, centralized versus decentralized translates into form prevailing over content. Where a computing machine is physically placed is not the issue. What is at issue is how to make computer systems more sensitive to the unique needs of an individual business function, thereby helping that function achieve its end goals for the business.

Consider what happened at a multibillion dollar corporation that decided to decentralize. It had the traditional, centralized business technology department. The department's staff thought its resources were inadequate; the users felt the department was unresponsive; senior management was sure the department wasn't helping the company achieve its goals.

After many hours of meetings, senior management finally agreed that decentralization was the answer, and the process began. Everyone was hopeful. But after two years, there were no significant changes. Even though computers had been moved out to "decentralized" locations, the same problems remained.

Well, what did they expect? They still had the same staff. They still had the same computer systems. They still had the same *thinking*. How could anything change?

Or consider a $500 million food chain. Various divisions were unhappy with the centralized business technology department, so corporate management decided to decentralize. At the last minute, my company was called in to determine if the scheme would work or not. We went to one division and asked, What will happen on Day One? How will decentralizing affect how you do business? Their answer was, Well, at least we'll have control. Another division immediately began buying its own computers; when we visited, we found they were recreating another centralized computing facility. Yet to this day, not a single one of the systems is up and running.

Having control is not the answer, nor is moving the computer center from one place to another. That's the old, centralized thinking. Neither one of these companies stopped to ask the more basic questions: What is our mission? How can computers help us achieve that mission?

The difference between centralized–decentralized computing and dispersed computing could be characterized like this. Centralized–decentralized computing is like a military tank, where a single engine drives the tank treads. Each tread may steer left or steer right, or react differently to the terrain, but there is only one power source applying brute force to the task. To translate, various business functions may use the computer's services or data in different ways, but all must draw those services or data from a single computer or organization.

Dispersed computing is more like the army's experimental spider-like, all-terrain climbing robot. Each leg has its own motor, and each leg senses the differences in terrain as the robot moves and climbs, either forward, backwards, or sideways. The robot responds to each differing condition as the condition requires. Similarly, user organizations can employ a dispersed computing technology in precisely the way that is best for them: creating their own systems, designing their own data bases, or setting task priorities to suit themselves.

*Distributed Computing.* This is another commonly used term in computing today, and one with which I strongly disagree. A popular college textbook on business data processing says that a distributed system is more flexible because it places computer power where it is needed. The author goes on to cite a company's distributed system that has a couple of hundred network-connected processors, thousands of terminals and printers, several hundred remote job entry stations, and hundreds of network processing systems at plant sites all over the world.

This suggests that the computer power is in the hands of the users, but that is not the case. This system, and many other so-called distributed systems like it, is nothing more than a geographically enormous centralized computing system. Distributed processing, in fact, is nothing more than remote processing, or remote data entry. Users simply pass data back and forth to the mainframe; control remains behind the glass walls of the centralized business technology department. Computer power is not distributed; the processors are all connected in a network. The users have no control over the computer; they are using terminals and remote job entry stations. Applications are chosen and managed by the network processing systems.

In a dispersed system, there would be no need to interconnect so many devices into such a single, complex scheme. Computer power is dispersed from the centralized computer in concentric rings, each with its own machines, its own applications, and its own needs.

## Dispersed Computing Is Resource Management

As I have pointed out again and again, simply moving machines from place to place does not alter the fact that centralized computing is still centralized dispensing of computer services. Dispersed computing is, in fact, resource management, which includes dispersing computers, dispersing applications, dispersing technological expertise, and dispersing innovation. We will take a close look at each, to see how you might manage your computer resource differently.

### Dispersing Computers

In dispersed computing, the mainframe still plays an important role. It performs tasks that influence a variety of functions and organizations in the company. However, specialized groups or functions are free to do their own computing using their own computers.

For example, one of our clients had established a computer-aided design (CAD) application on their mainframe. CAD, being a graphics system, draws a great deal of central processing unit (CPU) power. Within a year of installation, it became necessary to upgrade to a larger processor, an IBM 3081. The following year they had to upgrade again, this time to an IBM 3084. And it didn't stop there; the 3084 grew overloaded, and response time dropped. Our client appeared to be heading for serious problems.

With a dispersed system, engineers can do design work on their own smaller mainframe, mini, or micro without taxing the central computer. However, the central computer would still play an important role: supporting the novices and relatively small groups of users. And for the larger, more sophisticated users, the CAD drawing data base would be maintained in the central computer, so it could be shared between various engineering units. Meanwhile, smaller computers containing the real CAD design functionally would be dispersed to the user organizations. In this instance, groups of engineers are free to grow more proficient on the system as well as to innovate, without taking response time or functionality away from other users.

## Dispersing Applications

Once it's understood that computer hardware can be placed anywhere it's needed, the most important task is dispersing the application software. Again, the first and most important step is to figure out what the specific organizations and their users need to accomplish their work. Though this might seem simple, it often is not. The first tendency is to recreate a massive data base, which triggers the business technology people into thinking about larger processors, capacity planning, and the whole centralized scheme of things. It is far better to plan the applications in three stages:

- What must stay in the central data base.
- What works best at the organizational level.
- What works best at the individual, or ad hoc, level.

For example, a manufacturing organization thought it would need to replicate almost 70 percent of the data in the corporate data base for its planning and scheduling purposes. However, once we began working with them we found that what at first seemed to be a high quantity of data was really a high flowthrough; that is, material had to be tracked, but it moved through the plant very quickly. What's more, only 17 percent of this data needed to be stored in the corporate data base. At the organizational level, a relatively simple relational data base, accessed with a fourth-generation language, gave them all the computer power they needed.

## Dispersing Technical Expertise

Computers are not the only resource shared in a dispersed environment. The business technology department staff should also be dispersed. Say a group of CAD engineers wants to innovate, but needs system development assistance. Business technology can transfer or assign some of its talent to the CAD group for developing the new applications. Once that is done, they can help train users as well.

Two things are thus simultaneously accomplished. First, in a short while the business technology professional feels like a member of the user department, charged with helping the department become more productive. Second, a rapport is created between the users and the technologists that didn't exist before, dispelling a great deal of misunderstanding. In the end, both feel more productive.

We often forget that the business technology department, regardless of its shortcomings, is one of the firm's greatest resources. It is the repository for the firm's technical expertise; properly directed, it can be the driving force behind technological innovation. As such, the business technology staff needs to be valued and nurtured. If they need to make changes and adjustments in the way they do things, then management should lend its help, support, and encouragement in the process. If they are to help the corporation choose appropriate technologies, users and management must guide them. Senior management needs to take an active stance in this process, guiding and shaping business technology's role in helping the firm attain its goals. If the staff is locked into old, centralized ways of thinking, without management's help their culture may never change.

### Dispersing Innovation

Once computers and technical expertise are dispersed, innovation can begin. There are two kinds of innovation at work when it comes to computer technology. One is technological innovation related to the computer system itself, and the other is organizational innovation and its implications.

A common misconception is that innovation and productivity are antithetical. I feel nothing could be further from the truth. Technological innovation inspires people to find better, faster ways to do their work. In fact, both can occur simultaneously without diminishing the other. The two can work hand-in-hand if allowed to.

As I mentioned, the business technology department traditionally has been responsible for technological innovation, such as bringing new systems and procedures into the corporation. There is no reason that cannot occur, but there are three caveats.

The first is that innovation must benefit the users. Business technology is not the sole beneficiary of new techniques, machines, or improvements in computer services. Innovation, like any other corporate resource, must be planned with and approved by user groups.

Second, innovation must be done with senior management's involvement and approval. People must meet to discuss how the computer resource is managed and implemented, to assure that it is directed toward the business's goals and missions. There must be no more technology for technology's sake.

Third, innovation should occur in a dispersed manner. We must begin thinking of computers as an expendable resource. Prices have fallen dramatically, and in many cases it is cheaper to toss an entire computer system out and buy a new one than to convert the old computer's software.

In his essay "Of Innovations," Sir Francis Bacon wrote, "He that will not apply new remedies must expect new evils; for time is the greatest innovator." The real innovation is no longer occurring on the mainframe computer, which resides in the centralized business technology department. It will occur at the furthest dispersed points, as far away from the central computer as possible. If there is any doubt about this, consider the software industry. Mainframe software companies have watched their annual growth decline from over 30 percent to under 10 percent; microcomputer software companies are now growing at a 30 percent rate. Innovation is occurring on the microcomputers, the smaller machines, which are in the hands of the users.

Organizational innovation is less straightforward, but no less important. How and where does it occur? It is difficult to say, but one thing I can assure you: The more centralized the computing facility, the less innovation you will see. Innovation is highest at the most dispersed end of the computing spectrum. People simply must have the opportunity to work with the computer on their own terms. There is a payback for the business technology department as well, for the users may have useful suggestions for system improvement that would never occur to the business technology staff simply because they are not out there at the action centers.

How do you get organizational innovation going? It takes time. Again, it requires a major shift in thinking to allow the emergence of a whole new computing concept and culture, free from centralized control. In the new culture people don't care who is in control, so long as they have the computing resources they need.

### Planning Dispersed Computing

As we create a dispersed system, it's essential that it be well within a planned architecture. To the users, it may seem that computers are all over the company, willy-nilly, but senior management, departmental management, and business technology must orchestrate the plan. When dispersed computing is not well planned, decentralized computing is most often the result.

Under the dispersed approach, commonly about 20 percent of the users need to be tied to the mainframe. The remaining 80 percent infrequently need to connect with another computer, whether it is the mainframe or not. The challenge lies in how to disperse the computer power properly.

### How Much Does Dispersed Computing Cost?

If you take the actual cost of computers and their supporting staff, centralization will, on the face of things, appear to come in lower. But when you take into consideration the effect that poor computer performance has on the business—the ability to respond to the users' changing needs or the lost opportunities in meeting business objectives and goals—then the cost pendulum distinctly swings over to the dispersed computing side.

Assume the central computer facility is running at 97 percent capacity, and purchasing requests an additional functionality. The analyst says this will consume an extra 5 percent of the CPU, and thus the computer system will be running at 10 percent, or over capacity. One scenario is that the request is disapproved, so purchasing loses an opportunity to increase its productivity. Another scenario is that the application is approved, but business technology will need an additional CPU, which costs $3 million.

In a dispersed system, the purchasing department would simply acquire its own computer, at a cost of perhaps $120,000. Software might cost an additional $30,000, plus $100,000 in salary for two people to operate and maintain the system. That's $250,000 versus $3 million.

Furthermore, now purchasing can draw data from the central computer's data base into its own computer, such as data on material requirements. Once these data are automatically entered into the departmental computer, then purchasing activities, vendor analyses, and other functions are handled locally. As scheduled delivery dates are identified, they are passed back to the central computer, where they can be shared with other interested departments. This approach, in effect, offloads work from the central processors, improving response time and productivity throughout the company. All other centralized costs drop proportionately as well.

This is truly dispersed processing. We will still have mainframe computers, minicomputers, and everything in between. But we will *use* them differently, more efficiently, and perhaps more wisely. The highest degree of innovation will occur at user workstations, where the real productivity gains are manifested, not within the business technology department.

### The Future

Now is the time to begin this dispersing process. The hardware, software, and technology staff must be dispersed to the company. Keep the corporate data base and the accounting system where they are—where they should be. But give the users control over their own functional applications.

The most important point is this: Begin thinking differ-

ently about your computer resources. Business practices have
changed in your firm, and technology must support those
changes to obtain as many productivity gains as possible. Think
long and hard on this, and plan carefully. A well-planned strategy is required for implementing a dispersed computer architecture; it must be managed properly, with respect for the people
involved, and by keeping the company's goals firmly in mind.

Technology will continue to grow and evolve; it will
never regress. It may grow more transparent, but we will always
have computers, and people will always need to use them. It's
the way we *deliver* computer technology to the users that must
change and evolve. There is no one answer, no one solution to
this. But it is time you begin to think about it, and time to begin formulating a strategy to carry your firm into the future.

# 6

‎ꓹꓹ‎ꓹꓹ‎ꓹꓹ‎ꓹꓹ‎ꓹꓹ‎ꓹꓹ‎ꓹꓹ‎ꓹꓹ‎ꓹꓹ‎ꓹꓹ‎ꓹꓹ‎ꓹꓹ‎ꓹꓹ‎ꓹꓹ‎ꓹꓹ‎ꓹꓹ‎ꓹꓹ

# A View of Tomorrow's Systems Architecture

In the previous chapter, I explained the concept of dispersing computers throughout the organization. This is how tomorrow's system architecture will be deployed: in a computing environment where the users with the greatest need receive the most computer services. Dispersed computing requires a new architecture, to be sure, but it does not demand that we throw out everything we have and start anew. It is primarily, and most importantly, a new way of thinking about the computer resource.

What is meant by the term *system architecture?* It's the same process as designing a building. It is a set of design principles that defines a relationship of, and interaction between, various parts of a system or network of systems, including the organization of functions. System architecture starts with a look at the business as a whole to determine the best way computer technology can be used to support the business and its mission to produce its products better, faster, and cheaper. And it is not just looking at the individual functions, but the relationships between all the functions in the business.

You have probably heard many consultants, authors, and other practitioners advocate a specific way of doing something. In most cases, the person developed a solution to a problem

69

that worked in a particular situation, then extrapolated it into a system or methodology.

That is not my purpose here. I want to show you that the best computer system is a simple computer system. The way to achieve this is to disperse the computer power throughout the organization, moving applications away from the centralized computer and as close to the user as possible. The application strategy I present here is conceptual in nature. The method of implementing it into a system architecture can vary significantly, depending on the nature of the business or governmental body and its size. What works for a manufacturing company will not work the same way for a health maintenance organization. However, the elements inherent in the strategy are based on good, sound computer technology principles, and thus will work for most companies with appropriate adaptation.

### The Need for a New Strategy

Most companies do not have an overall system architecture. If they do, it usually is a patchwork of current technologies serving the existing, time-worn approach to applications. The inherent problem with this approach to a system architecture is that it assumes that those ten- to fifteen-year-old applications are satisfactory. Thus, whatever exists becomes, by default, the foundation for further architectural developments.

This assumption—that what we are doing today is satisfactory for the future—is a critical error in judgment. Whenever any kind of computer technology decision needs to be made, the first consideration is analyzing the effectiveness of today's system and applications.

To do this, we must go through the process of reflecting on future requirements while, at the same time, evaluating the supportability of our current direction. Throughout this process, these are the kinds of questions to which you should be seeking answers.

• Is what we are doing today maximizing computer technology to the extent that, if we continue in the same direction, the company will derive significant benefits?

• Are we effectively responding to and servicing the needs of the computer technology users within the company, and will we be able to support them properly in the future?

• How does the user community view business technology's support and contribution in supplying this technology? Are the users helped to achieve their goals and the goals of the business? If we continue in the same direction, how will users perceive business technology in the future?

These questions are intended to help you evaluate the future consequences of continuing in the same direction you are going today. The point here is that if no formal planning went into the system architecture your firm has in place today, then it is incumbent upon you to ensure that such an error does not occur again. No one needs to be blamed if there is no system architecture; as John Locke wrote in his "Essay Concerning Human Understanding":

> Error is not the fault of our knowledge, but a mistake of our judgment. . . . Those who cannot carry a train of consequences in their heads; nor weigh exactly the preponderancy of contrary proofs and testimonies . . . may be easily misled to assent to positions that are not probable.

## Future Systems Architecture

Any future systems architecture must address three different missions: company needs for system integration of functions and data, organizational or departmental needs for applications that are responsive to their unique internal requirements, and an application environment that provides individual users with the tools they need to accomplish their work. I call these three levels of systems architecture *enterprise level systems, departmental level systems,* and *ad hoc level systems.*

*Enterprise Level Systems.* These systems maintain the primary management and operational data that cut across the company as a whole. Enterprise level systems should be limited to

Figure 1. Application System Hierarchy.

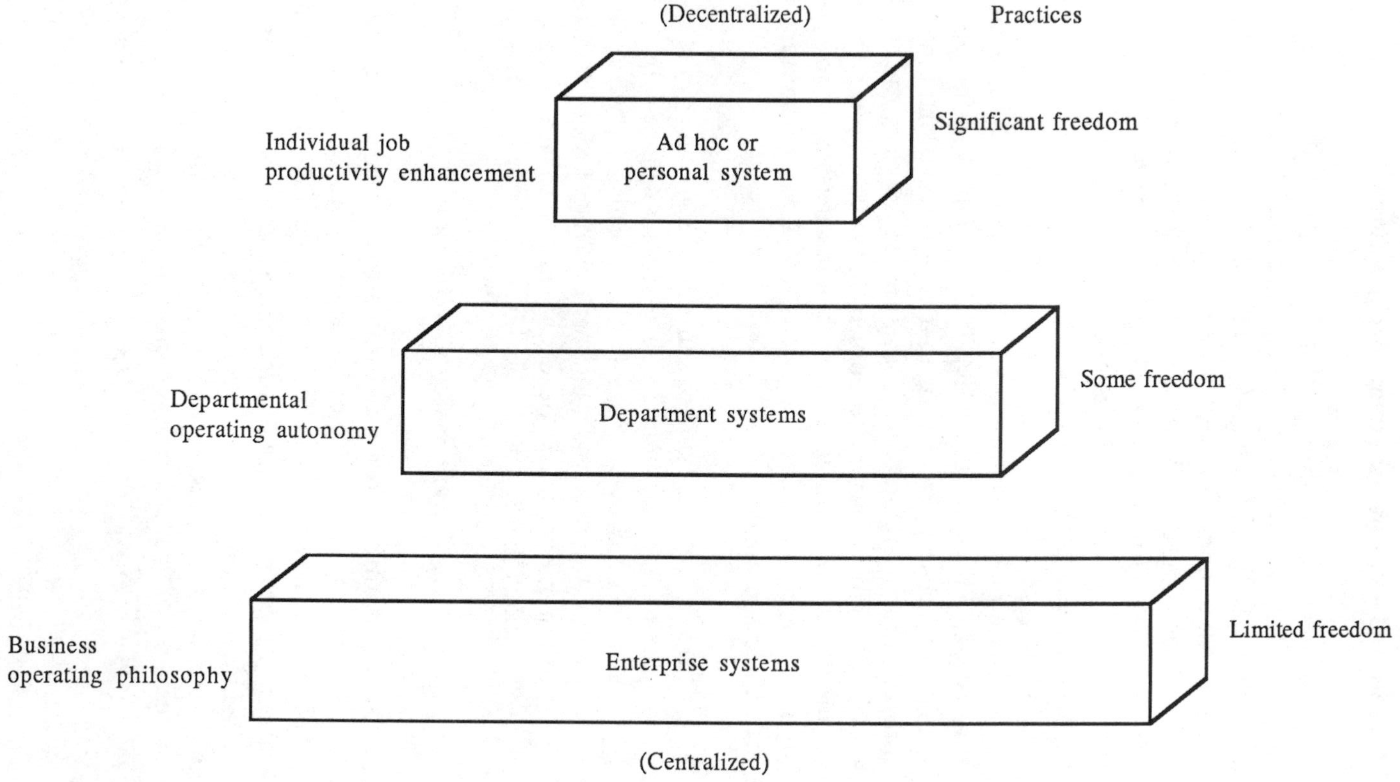

Practices

(Decentralized)

Significant freedom

Ad hoc or personal system

Individual job productivity enhancement

Some freedom

Department systems

Departmental operating autonomy

Limited freedom

Enterprise systems

(Centralized)

Business operating philosophy

only processes that integrate key business functions. These systems are both a transporter of data between entities and a maintainer of data that are shared between multiple entities. I view an enterprise level system as the primary means of achieving control between various organizational entities within a business unit. This assures that a common operating philosophy is achieved.

Notice that enterprise level systems normally are not involved in creating data or in determining the manner in which data are used. These activities are best performed at the other two levels of the system hierarchy. This allows an appropriate balance between control at the enterprise system level and maximum independence and flexibility of processing at the departmental or ad hoc level of the hierarchy. By taking this approach, you will greatly reduce the complexity which would result from the mixing of departmental requirements with overall company requirements.

*Departmental Level Systems.* These are systems that are placed within a departmental or even an organizational unit within a department. Their purpose is to achieve the unique objectives of that entity. For example, consider how different the needs are for processing, managing, and controlling a purchasing organization versus a marketing department or a manufacturing organization. Though these various departments may share some data, most of their data processing can be self-contained and should be treated that way. These organizations should have the authority and responsibility to select and implement their own solutions to satisfy their individual objectives.

Departmental level computer application processes deal with a variety of situations and special cases, which makes the application software design relatively complex. This complexity should be addressed by those individuals who are familiar with the functions their departments perform. Further, the definition and implementation of data that are originated in the department should be their responsibility as well. The software design and maintenance demands of department application functions are thus isolated from the enterprise level applications.

The system hierarchy concept suggests that large central programming staffs may no longer be required. Some of these people can be moved out to the departments to directly support them. This will give departmental managers not only the responsibility but also the capability to use their computers as they deem necessary.

Decisions about the number and capacity of the company's computers are more manageable when the system hierarchy concept is applied. Growth in central computer capacity is more easily controlled when it is no longer driven by departmental processing demands. Computer resource needs at the departmental level, on the other hand, are influenced mainly by the number of terminals and workstations these computers must support. With a dispersed computing approach, functional managers find that they can decide for themselves whether to increase computer capacity or to buy more terminals, because they alone make the terminal response time versus computer cost tradeoffs. Their computer cost decisions are not compromised by priority or peak processing demands of other users. Departmental managers are put in a position to better control their work.

*Ad Hoc Level Systems.* These are not systems in the usual sense of the word, but rather a variety of tools and techniques that permit individual users to set up their own systems. As I have said before, we find the most innovation at this level of the architecture, so these systems have the fewest controls and permit the greatest freedom.

Here we find a high proliferation of personal computers, personal productivity software, English-like natural languages, and fourth-generation languages that tie into relational data base management systems. Often we find software and other capabilities provided by the company's information center, which allows desktop microcomputers to act as on-line terminals to other computers or data bases.

Even though I say control is slight at this level, it is important that the users adhere to conventions established by the business technology department for the architecture as a whole. If the corporate standard is set for IBM PCs and compatibles, or the approved data base software is, say, dBase III, then all users must adhere to those products. This facilitates a degree of compatibility for future systems planning, which would be essential if, for example, a local area network were installed. It also means data can easily be distributed and shared. And last but not least, it facilitates learning efforts, because an experienced user can help the novices.

The enterprise, departmental, and ad hoc systems together comprise the integrated application environment of the future. The goal always is to move the technology out. A well-planned, well-executed, dispersed architecture is essential for using computer technology as an enabling device and moving the business aggressively into the future.

## System Architecture Examples

Consider how a dispersed architecture might work in a large engineering manufacturing company. Figure 2 portrays the relationship between enterprise and departmental systems as products are developed and manufactured.

From a computer system viewpoint, the enterprise system is comprised of those applications that capture and maintain data defining the product and used directly in its production. Departmental systems may use enterprise data in the performance of their own functions. However, the key idea here is that the results of certain departmental functions are fed back into enterprise data files; other data produced in departmental functions are outside the domain of the enterprise data base and should be under the control of the responsible department. Data extraction, processing, and feedback elements are represented in Figure 2 as "process loops."

A guideline I use in allocating functions between enter-

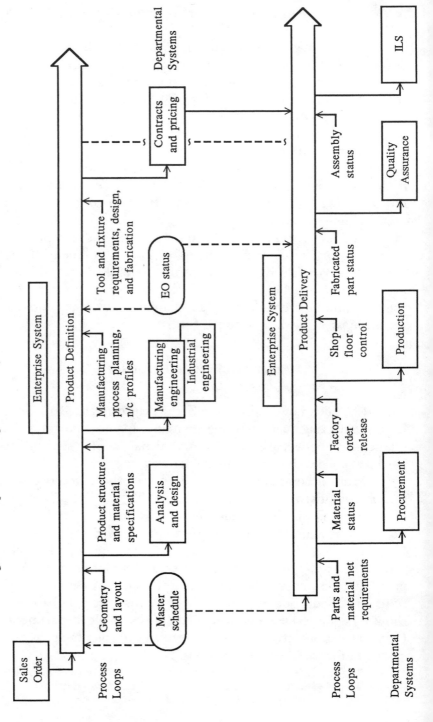

Figure 2. Enterprise and Departmental System Relationships: Data and Process Flow.

prise and departmental systems is to keep a particular process in the domain of departmental systems, unless a strong case can be made for its inclusion in the enterprise system. You should keep the processes included in the enterprise system to a minimum, so that the enterprise system's purpose is not diluted. The enterprise system in this example has two essential reasons for existence: to cause changes in master schedules to be reflected in individual product definition-delivery schedules as quickly as possible and with utmost accuracy, and to reflect the intent of engineering orders in all processes as quickly as they occur while assuring that compliance has occurred for each of the affected item serial numbers and at the intended location(s).

When viewing this same process from a data ownership standpoint, each department is assigned full responsibility for entry of designated information into the enterprise data base. The system's inputs and outputs will be fully controlled within the enterprise system. Data extracted from enterprise system operations are further processed by departmental systems, generally including preparation of individualized reports. These departmental systems may have separate data files for use with their own internal transactions and for processes occurring outside the enterprise system.

Consider another example, a large conglomerate. The general manager our firm worked with developed something he called the level of maximum management, or LOMM, concept. With LOMM, the idea was to move data away from the central data base and out to where appropriate management could make the best use of it. By and large, this was at the departmental level. The general manager understood that his company had a significant amount of intercommerce, so there should be one central accounting department to control, balance, and maintain all the accounting data, overhead, and distribution of burden to direct costs. However, each division or department should be able to use that data as it applies to its function, and even add to it, as necessary.

The LOMM concept was based on the fact that the old, outmoded, centralized computing concept was not helping this business get its job done. In his report to senior management, the general manager cited a number of problems:

- The user's application programs were intertwined with the central system's data base. Everyone was trying to use a massive data base for his or her own operational purposes.
- Use of common applications coupled with a single data base necessitates a single solution shared by many users, which results in compromise for users whose business operations may not be the same. It requires constant, continuing education of all users when changes are made to accommodate another's business needs, and it results in large users' requirements overriding and dictating to the others.
- The combination of application complexity and extensive data manipulation leads directly to slow response for the users. The old system's design caused delays in servicing concurrent requests for data when these data were stored at the same place in the system's files.

This general manager concluded that connection is not communication, and as more users were connected, the system would begin to overload. He also reported that centralized data processing in a high-volume environment is not responsive to the needs at the level of maximum management.

As we began working with this company, a number of solutions to the problems emerged. First, move operating data out to the managers who need it and work with it the most, so they can manage more efficiently. Second, transfer as much of the data manipulation and reporting functions out of the central business technology department as possible and into the functional division or department. Third, don't throw out the central data services, but use them instead to maintain standardized and explicit meanings of data shared among central functions and the LOMMs. Fourth, strictly separate centralized data processing functions from divisional or departmental computer functions. Fifth, encourage an environment in which business technology provides support and helps develop innovative computing solutions for LOMMs. Figure 3 shows how the LOMM architecture works at this company.

The beauty of the dispersed architecture is that it can be implemented in the manner appropriate to a particular firm. And it does not always require discarding the old to begin. In many cases, once the new architecture has been determined, implementation can start through appropriate interconnects to the old systems, and over time, system replacement will occur.

We took the following approach with a check processing and credit card approval company. In their business, once they approve a check they are liable for payment if it bounces. The claims at this firm were primarily handled manually, with some computer assistance, and numbered approximately ninety thousand at any given time. There was no way to keep up under a work load like this, and the claims group had been trying to get business technology support for over two years. Business technology lacked sufficient computer and development resources to support the claims group, and a larger processor and more mass storage would be required if they were to take on the job.

Our recommendation was to install a separate computer for the claims group, using a fourth-generation language to write the application. Within six months, the backlog was cleared up and the group was able to keep current on a day-to-day basis. This was due in large part to the fact that we approached the situation as a stand-alone application, which in fact it was. There was no need to involve central business technology and the mainframe computer. In fact, an application like this is a small job for a supermicrocomputer.

### Planning the Implementation

Moving from one architectural base to another is a demanding task, yet can we logically turn our backs on the task? If change is really required or essential, should we not, at a minimum, take time to analyze our business and computer technology environment, determine the impact of moving to a dispersed environment, and judge at that time the merits and the

Figure 3. LOMM Architecture and Configurations.

## LOMM Architecture

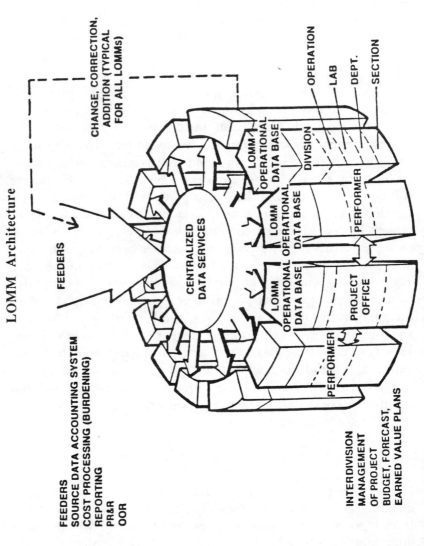

FEEDERS
SOURCE DATA ACCOUNTING SYSTEM
COST PROCESSING (BURDENING)
REPORTING
PR&R
OOR

CHANGE, CORRECTION,
ADDITION (TYPICAL
FOR ALL LOMMs)

FEEDERS

CENTRALIZED DATA SERVICES

LOMM OPERATIONAL DATA BASE

LOMM OPERATIONAL DATA BASE

LOMM OPERATIONAL DATA BASE

LOMM OPERATIONAL DATA BASE

DIVISION
OPERATION
LAB
DEPT.
SECTION

PERFORMER

PERFORMER

PROJECT OFFICE

PERFORMER

INTERDIVISION
MANAGEMENT
OF PROJECT
BUDGET, FORECAST,
EARNED VALUE PLANS

LOMM Configurations

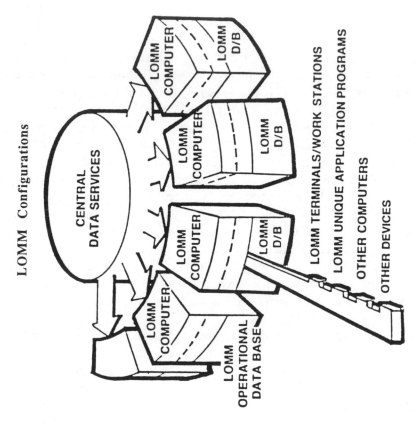

CENTRAL DATA SERVICES

LOMM COMPUTER

LOMM D/B

LOMM COMPUTER

LOMM D/B

LOMM COMPUTER

LOMM D/B

LOMM COMPUTER

LOMM OPERATIONAL DATA BASE

LOMM TERMINALS/WORK STATIONS

LOMM UNIQUE APPLICATION PROGRAMS

OTHER COMPUTERS

OTHER DEVICES

*Source:* Used with kind permission of TRW Inc.

costs? Quite often what at first may seem like a massive change with extraordinary cost implications, may turn out to be achievable when you factor in what you are spending today with questionable results. If the subject of moving forward to a new architecture is approached right, you may be favorably surprised.

First, you must approach the situation as a form of strategic planning, in the same way you approach new product development or any other long-range plans. When making changes of this type, you have to consider how you would like to see your firm performing some number of years—three, five, or ten —from now. You want to begin a systematic migration from the "as-is" to the "to-be." It is a gradual, not a sudden, change.

Second, I have mentioned the matter of costs before. The delta cost is whatever you would spend, over and above what you would normally be spending, if the new plan never existed. Look back over the past five years and note how your business technology costs have been increasing. Now take the same rate of growth and apply it to the future. That figure represents what your costs will likely be five years from now. Why not take that rate of expenditure and apply it toward new hardware, software, and people costs that further the new architecture? You're going to spend the money one way or the other; why not get the return you want from it? In the bargain, you may find that your delta cost is actually lower than if you had continued in the old ways.

Third, if you decide to move immediately ahead toward a new architecture, you might think you need to increase the size of the systems development staff. That is not necessarily true. In many cases, half the staff is involved in maintenance and upkeep, while the other half is working on future enhancements. By assigning part of this staff to work on activities that develop and promote the new architecture, additional staff may not be required. You may also want to examine all the backlogged projects the staff is working on, assign priorities to some, and eliminate others. In short, you may end up changing the work load or the mix, but the total number of staff required to meet your company's needs remains the same.

My intention is not to oversimplify the process or mislead

you into thinking that, at certain times, there won't be additional costs or manpower requirements. But on the other hand,
you should not accept the philosophy that anything new requires spending more money and hiring new people. If you
think carefully about the situation, there are many ways to re-
direct resources without spending additional funds. I am convinced that if you perform an analysis, you may find that
you're able to achieve many of the objectives required to implement tomorrow's architecture with a minimal increase (and in
some cases virtually no increase) in delta cost.

# 7

╖╜╖╜╖╜╖╜╖╜╖╜╖╜╖╜╖╜╖╜╖╜╖╜╖╜╖╜╖╜╖╜╖╜╖╜

# Planning and Creating
# Productive Information Systems

Harold Laski, one of England's leading twentieth-century econ-
omists, once said, "We must plan our civilization or we must
perish." In like fashion, companies that lack an overall plan or
strategy for their computer system architecture seriously jeop-
ardize their chances for growth and success in the future.

An architecture helps a company determine how, and in
what form, computer technology will be implemented to achieve
the firm's goals. When I go into a company, one of my first
questions is, Do you have a system architecture? The answer is
invariably yes, we do; however, in viewing that architecture, I
find it relates primarily to a hardware or a communications network. Such an architecture addresses only how the technology
is connected, but not necessarily the needs of the users or the
business itself. I ask further, How will the technology be used? I
am told that the users will be better able to share information
and to communicate with one another. If I ask why they need
to do this, or how this will benefit the company, the answers
become considerably more vague.

What's the problem here? Quite simply, there is no strategy for the computer systems architecture. When I say strategy,
I mean *the science or art of planning and directing activities to*

84

*achieve a desired goal.* It is difficult to use the technology properly when there is no business purpose in mind. I have no problem with the idea of a hardware or communications network architecture, nor with users communicating with each other. In fact, both are essential. But these are the means, not the end. My point is that without a strategy that produces a desired business goal, the technology is going to waste.

Historically, the firm's goals and the business technology department's goals have not been the same. A primary reason is that the business people have never taken the time to develop a true system architecture strategy that responds to the overall needs of the business. This is an essential first step that must be taken before we can begin using technology as an enabling device.

In Chapter One I spoke of the productivity crisis, and how computer technology has come up short in helping U.S. business achieve significant productivity gains. Without a strategy for deploying the computer resource and a computer system architecture that addresses business needs, the business will continue to flounder and stagnate.

We are at a major crossroads in deciding how computer technology is going to be used in the future. The problems are detailed in frequent cover stories in every business magazine. You must make a decision about your company's computer resource. Don't say you can't afford to make the time or the monetary commitment; you can't afford not to. The problem is already costing you hundreds of thousands, perhaps millions of dollars a year in lost opportunity and overhead. Let's begin to focus your business technology expenditures on those things that benefit the business. Now is the time to act and do it right. Let's be sure that the strategy we employ and the energy we expend will truly help us reach our business goals.

## Old Planning Techniques

It's not that we have been without a planning strategy or methodology in the past; it's simply that the methodologies of yesterday and today are woefully inadequate. Their purpose, for the most part, was simply to help perform tasks more quickly, which at one time was probably considered a "productivity gain." But they cannot help us implement a future architecture that addresses the changing needs of the users or that helps us produce our product or service better, faster, or cheaper.

Many of the old methodologies were, in the parlance of business technology, "information-driven," such as IBM's Business Systems Planning (BSP). Others incorporated such things as "functional activity models" with "information flow models" that created "business models." The process began when the programmers–analysts diagrammed the business operation, noting where every piece of paper or scrap of information came from and went to. This took months and months, and was often frustrating and exhausting for those involved. In many cases, this data collection aspect became so complex that it would require a miracle to design a system that accounted for every need.

Perhaps the greatest drawback to diagramming business functions and activities is that *it only accounts for where a business is right now.* It doesn't consider where the company is going, and so is doomed to be out of date before it is even implemented.

In most cases, the concentration is on "information." This supports the prevailing myth in the business technology culture that information is the computer's end product. Though the various ways in which computers are able to manipulate and deliver "information" are fascinating to business technology personnel, there are no inherent productivity gains that benefit the business in such activities.

To underscore my point, consider this description of a seminar for executives:

> This program will give executives a solid basis for directing the implementation of technology for the information age in which we live. Meetings will focus on devising strategies for controlling the costs of handling information.

There are probably some useful and worthwhile techniques presented in a seminar like this, but it's still yesterday's thinking. It promotes what I call ephemeral planning, because it makes everyone feel good for a few fleeting moments, but can rarely be implemented in the day-to-day business world. If we are going to see the benefits of computer technology as an enabling device that truly benefits the company, we must begin what I call sensible planning: not what we'd ideally like to have in a perfect world, but what is realistic and achievable.

One more point: Conventional planning strategies are concerned with managing the data we have collected and plan to collect. These strategies assume we will continue to amass more and more data on more and more functions, and never address what I consider of greater importance. If computer technology can be properly deployed, *is it not conceivable that we could reduce the amount of data we collect and retain, and perhaps eliminate some redundant functions as well?*

### Developing a New Planning Approach

There are certain points in a company's business cycle when extraordinary effort is required to make a major shift or change in the way things are done. At these points, standard methods for creating change are not adequate. New approaches must be sought. If you have read this far, then you probably realize you are at this point with your computer technology. Further, I assume you want to explore those new approaches. How to begin? By bringing the firm's movers and shakers together to plan the strategy.

*The Skunk Works.* Many years ago, Lockheed came up with the idea of gathering a team of people together in some off-site location for brainstorming new products. The term *skunk* comes from the notion that these people are isolated, and that no one wants to be around them. It was an immediate success at Lockheed, and now many other companies have adopted the concept. Great ideas almost always emerge. One of the most famous skunk works projects was creating the MV-8000 superminicomputer at Data General, which was chronicled in Tracy Kidder's Pulitzer Prize–winning book, *The Soul of a New Machine.*

I believe the skunk works is the best environment for tackling something as important as a new computer system architecture. First of all, it allows the team to break away physically and mentally from the everyday corporate culture. And moreover, it gives them freedom to identify new ways in which computer technology can be used to support the business and help it thrive. The skunk works allows people to get rid of their inhibitions and innovate without restrictions. The goal is an environment where they can think and talk without the conventional business constraints.

Senior management should demonstrate their support, and must remain visible and involved throughout the skunk works. This is important because it shows your confidence and trust in them. The teams need that, because they are changing the way computer technology is going to be used, and thus changing some fundamental ways you do business. Involvement says you are willing to accept the risks in giving them this assignment. Without that outward sign of confidence, it will be more difficult for the team to innovate or to take the risks the project needs. They must feel confident, inspired, and secure.

As their leader, senior management must initiate the skunk works project and give the team its mission and focus. Skunk works participants must be clear and precise about their task; no one should think this is just another bull-shooting session or a low-level busy-work project. It must be clear that change will emerge. The team must have access to the firm's goals for the next five to ten years. The team must understand senior management's thinking and strategy in planning those goals. If they can grasp how that thinking came about, they have a much better chance of turning those goals into reality.

Depending on the size and complexity of the company, it may take three to six months for the skunk works to create its plan for the new system architecture. The team must understand that the project requires their full attention for the duration, no matter how long that is.

*The Composition of the Team.* The members of the skunk works should be people respected by their departments and the rest of the company. These people should be in a responsible line capacity, people who are committed "doers." The ideal mix is two-thirds line people from the user organizations, and one-third technology people.

The line people should be from different departments and functions throughout the company, and should be people who represent their organization and can speak for them. You want departmental line people who understand the business. You want operational people—those who meet the customers and are involved with the firm's product.

You do not want staff people who are steeped in procedures. Nor do you want backroom people who are interested in data for data's sake. You want the people who make the difference in the company.

From the technology side, you want people who are perceptive and can think in conceptual terms. These should be people who are clear thinkers and problem solvers, not those mired in yesterday's technology. They should have a broad understanding of the technology and its uses and applications, but not necessarily detailed knowledge, for that can be assigned.

*The Leader.* The skunk works leader should be someone who embraces the concept of technology as an enabling device, who is able to create an open and frank discussion environment, and who is not encumbered by company politics. He or she should be a senior manager who understands the business in its broadest perspective, and who is highly respected by both peers and management.

In one company my firm worked with, a group from senior management jointly developed a list of senior manager candidates to head the skunk works team. The man they chose was the director of manufacturing engineering, an up-and-coming executive. High on the list of qualifications was his understanding of the business, the respect he had from peers and senior management, and his ability to give others the guidance and direction they needed. Moreover, he was known for his skill in breaking logjams with organizations that, from time to time, were reluctant to provide needed support. He proved to be a good choice, and led his skunk works team to an admirable success in creating his company's new system architecture.

*Where the Team Works.* To be truly effective, the skunk works team should meet in an off-site environment. "Off-site" means far enough away from the daily operating environment to avoid constant interruptions about everyday matters. The actual place the team meets may be a conference room in the far corner of one of your current buildings, in a rented trailer or the company apartment, or in a meeting room at an inn or hotel.

The team members should have only the task at hand before them: planning and designing a new system architecture. The corporate culture drives us to certain preordained conclusions, and the team must break free of them if it is going to innovate. There are constant interruptions in our daily routines for phone calls and supposedly important messages, even at the most tightly-closed-door meeting. All these influences and interruptions must be eliminated for the skunk works to be successful.

The team comes and goes to work every day at the off-site location, just as if they were going to the office. Even three weeks is a long time for people to be away from their normal jobs, let alone three months. Participants often grow anxious about what is going on in their absence. Some may feel they will lose their positions to competitors if they're away too long. They must feel assured that their positions are not in jeopardy. In some cases, it may be necessary to let the team go to their offices one day a week. Be aware, however, that this creates a mind shift and may slow down the creative process.

There is no question that the company pays a price by sacrificing these people for the duration of the skunk works. But there is a payback as well. First, the new system architecture will be significantly more appropriate in supporting and advancing the business. Second, skunk works members, ostensibly the rising stars in the firm, receive a broad education in the combined aspects of business and technology. This unquestionably valuable experience puts them in a strong position to offer additional benefits to the company for a long time.

## Developing the New System Architecture

Once the team is formed, the work begins in earnest. Almost. To be realistic, not all skunk works team members will be available immediately. Most will need a little time to transfer their responsibilities to others while they are gone. This need not deter the start-up phase, however. There are many preparatory steps that need to be taken so the team can work effectively and efficiently once things are in full swing.

For example, let's say the project length has been set for six months. The first two months can be designated as preparation time, and the remaining four months as the actual skunk works project. Under such a plan, the two most important tasks during this period are establishing goals and building the business model.

*Establishing Goals.* Of all the skunk works activities, setting goals is the most important. If the goals are inadequate in the beginning, they will produce inadequate results at the end. They should be broad, general goals, but not easy ones; each should require a lot of thinking and hard work for the team. The goal-setters shouldn't be immediately concerned about whether or not the team can actually achieve the goals they set; rather, they should be good, desirable goals that are potentially achievable. One company, a diversified manufacturing concern we helped to develop a system architecture, set these goals for their skunk works team:

- Reduce the total cost of the divisions' direct and indirect nontouch labor by 30 percent.
- Reduce the full-scale product development schedule spans by 33 percent, and initial production spans prior to full production by 50 percent.
- Reduce internally generated changes to product definition by 75 percent.
- Improve the time span for incorporating changes by 50 percent.
- Improve shop floor direct-touch labor and equipment costs by 25 percent.

- Reduce the factory work-in-progress inventory by 50 percent.
- Facilitate improved information exchange standards and practices between the company and vendors, other contractors, and the customers.

Any skunk works team member examining these goals would have no doubt about what the team's objectives were. Equally important, goals like these demand that people look at the computer in an entirely different way: as an enabling technology for achieving the goals set forth. And with such specific goals, computer technology will be used, not in a purposeless manner, but with a strong, directed mission.

I learned this lesson the hard way. Back in the mid-1960s, I was asked to head a project to develop an automated production control and material *management information system.* And that's exactly what I did. Furthermore, when we completed the design we offered it to the president with great pride. We explained how the system was going to reduce inventory by 10 percent. We showed how the time to build a product would be shortened by five days. Best of all, we said, the new system would produce tons of "information" that would help to manage and control various processes.

After spending more than an hour listening to our presentation, this patient and polite man quietly complimented us on the exquisite design we had created. Then, less quietly, he told us we were  not to continue with the project. "If this company is going to be in business five years from now," he said, "we must reduce inventory by 30 percent and the time it takes to build the product must be reduced by forty-five days. That's what we need, and as for the information, if some is available, well, it might be nice."

We went away, properly admonished, to reconsider what we had done. Two months later, we went back into the president's office and made quite a different presentation. Our new system was far less complex than the previous one, produced quite a lot less "information," and met every goal he asked for.

Bold, clearly stated business goals are essential prerequisites if the skunk works team is to develop a new computer system architecture. And these goals are not simply to automate a manual function or, worse yet, to create another information system. These goals are to be developed by the skunk works team, working with senior management. During the first two months, the team might meet once a week to agree upon the goals.

In my dealings with companies, it's interesting to note that senior management often knows intuitively what has to be done for the business to remain competitive and healthy in the future. What is often difficult is getting them to articulate or convey it to others. In any case, once the goals are set, it is the skunk works team's responsibility to develop a strategy for achieving and implementing them.

*Building the Business Model.* During the same period, one or two of the team members are permanently assigned the task of building a high-level model of today's business practices. This is referred to as the "as-is" architecture model. Several of the business technology department staff may be assigned to this group on a temporary basis to assist in the definition. The "as-is" model is necessary as a tool to help the entire team when they meet later, on a full-time basis, to discuss the overall aspects of, and the interactions between, various business functions.

### The Full-Time Team Involvement

The first month of full-time involvement is hard on the team. It is also a chaotic time. People are getting used to one another, and trying to become comfortable away from their normal work. They have to adjust to spending day after day together, often in one room. They want structure and duties, which are not forthcoming unless they themselves create them.

There is also a lot of negativism at first. As the discussions begin and people start making suggestions, you hear a lot of we-can't-do-that or they-won't-let-us or that-can't-be-done comments. These are simply excuses people sometimes make up to justify flaws in the system.

This is when the leader begins to make his or her presence felt. He or she has to give the team permission to break rules, knock down defenses, and be innovative and creative. Unfortunately, the leader also becomes the team's scapegoat for many personal or corporate shortcomings. It's a tough position to be in, and very difficult to do successfully. At times, it's almost like conducting a group therapy session. This is why it is important to have a skilled leader who understands the business *and* the technology, and who knows how to lead people in this type of process. Often, it helps to bring someone in from outside the corporation. You want to do the skunk works just once, and do it right the first time.

After a while people have vented their anger and the inhibitions are gone. Gradually, they learn that there is no one there to tell them they can't do something, and if they want to do it, they can. The way this usually happens is someone lights a spark and the whole team takes off. The realization sinks in that they are in charge, they are the change agents. People loosen up, and the real communication begins. Now anything is possible, such as a computer architecture that works for them. They are on their way to becoming what I term *architecturists.*

## Technology Exploration

It is important that every member of the skunk works understand computer technology. In the early stage, let them explore computer technology in a free-wheeling fashion. Let them talk about the computers the firm currently uses. Let them talk about trends, new products, and new technologies until they are comfortable with them and understand them.

Often, the business people will be asking most of the questions and the technology people will be doing most of the answering. Let this happen. They may want to discuss artificial intelligence, relational data bases, parallel processing, or local area networks. Let them go into as much detail as they want about designing, creating, and engineering computer systems, until they are thoroughly satisfied.

At this point, the leader or an appointed architecturist will ask, If you could, how would you do things differently? And it's at this point that you begin learning how to create the new system architecture. Often the question has to be asked again and again, punctuated with, Yes, but what if . . . But the answers are invaluable.

One thing you learn during this stage is that most of your firm's departments and organizations are islands of automation. Even though they are connected to the central computer, they don't interact very much. Moreover, you learn the business technology department is an island, too; there is very little co-ordination in either data, functions, or ideas, and even less sharing with other departments.

It's important to keep these discussions moving ahead, for in time the team itself will recognize these islands and will want to overcome the isolation. The leader should continue asking questions about what is there and what isn't, probing until they find out what is missing and what is needed. The skunk works is creating the fertile ground in which to begin growing the new system architecture.

This exploration stage generally takes two months. Once completed, it is time for them to begin conceptualizing and designing the new system architecture.

*"As-Is" and "To-Be" Architecture.* The business people start by discussing business practices. They explain the nature of their work and what they want to accomplish. This is a fairly general discussion. For example, they may say they want to capture these or those data, and combine them with something else. They may say they want to automate a particular function or add a graphics workstation.

The technologist ventures opinions on what can or cannot be done. Gradually, the issues begin sorting themselves out. What emerges is an optimistic vision of the future in which a new, simpler, more flexible computer system seems possible. The technologist sees the promise of computers working more efficiently and harmoniously, systems that can be easily changed when necessary. The business people see the possibility of computers that adapt to the way they do their work, that permit growth and changes in the organization, and that serve the firm's missions and goals.

The subject of these early discussions is what I call the "as-is" and the "to-be" architectures: what we have now and what we want to have tomorrow. The reason for discussing the "as-is" architecture is to create a broader understanding of how the business operates today, and to locate the weak points. The "to-be" architecture is developed into a broad schema of what the future could be if technology is appropriately deployed. Now we have an architecture that marries business goals and computer technology.

This is a significant event at the skunk works. People feel they have accomplished something, and have come up with a new, promising, viable alternative to the complex, frustrating rat's nest computer system they now have. It is an achievement, and when it's accomplished, the members have indeed become architecturists.

*The New Architecture.* The next stage is to open discussions about the new architecture. The team must keep its focus sharply on how the new architecture will help the company achieve the goals the skunk works addressed. There is a great deal of enthusiasm and interest at this point. The team feels that it has earned its stripes, so to speak, and now they are ready to design the new system.

The work is broken into two phases. The first phase is developing the architectural concepts, and then thinking through their various impacts on the organization. Many issues cannot be resolved, but the important thing is to keep the discussion moving toward a new system architecture.

At the point when the team feels they have a preliminary architecture defined, they should prepare a report for senior management. This should explain how the new system architecture will form a solution to the goals with which the team was charged.

In the next phase, the team members must turn their ideas into a reality that can be implemented. First, they must study senior management's critique and comments, and locate the plan's strengths and weaknesses. Then they must revise and refine the plan, over and over if necessary, until they come up with a legitimate, final architecture.

The final stage of the skunk works involves writing a report to senior management that includes the following items:

- *The system architecture,* which explains the strategy for dispersing computer technology, how the functional or organizational applications will perform, and their relationship to other applications and processes.
- *Organizational impact.* This section deals with the functional realignments within the company that are necessary to fulfill the new architecture's mission. It also includes an impact analysis of these changes.
- *Computer hardware, software, and communications network architecture.* The team must explain how to develop the high-level technical architecture that will support the new system. This portion of the report describes where the computer hardware (whether centralized or dispersed) will be located, the interconnections between the hardware and the communications networks, and identifies the implementation policy and standardization requirements.
- *Computer technology delivery support requirements.* This section deals with the organizational aspects of delivering the new system architecture. It covers what should be centralized, what functions should be dispersed, and how these various functions will interact in the future.
- *Costs and benefits.* This section explains, in broad estimates, the costs associated with achieving the new architecture, the benefits the business stands to gain, and how those benefits relate to the original goals the skunk works was charged with.
- *Migration plan.* Here an overall scenario is developed that recommends how to move from the "as-is" to the "to-be" architecture.

The process for developing a system architecture is summarized in Figure 4. The process is neither complex nor new. It

**Figure 4. System Architecture Development Process.**

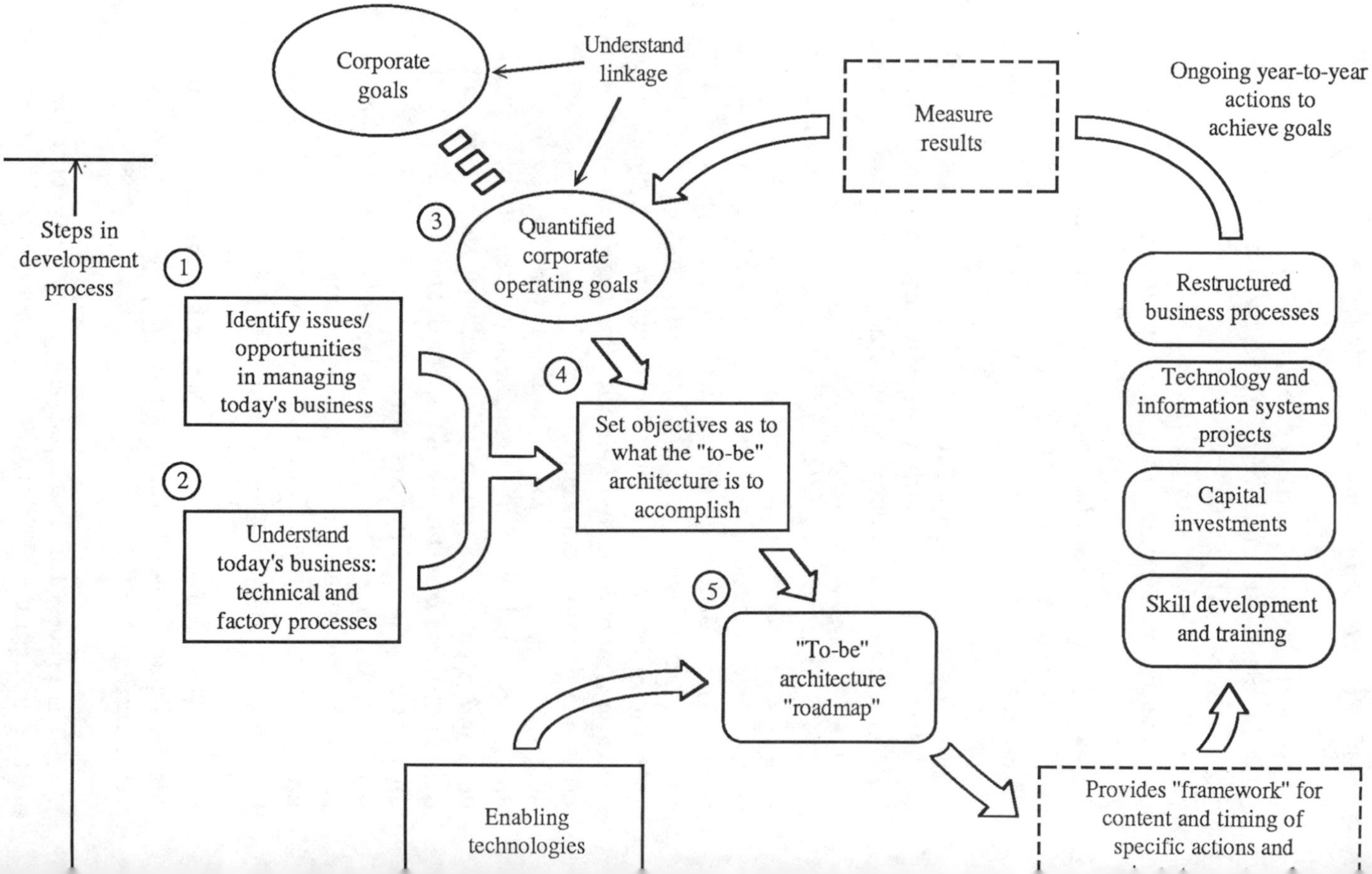

Steps in development process

1. Identify issues/opportunities in managing today's business

2. Understand today's business: technical and factory processes

Corporate goals

Understand linkage

3. Quantified corporate operating goals

4. Set objectives as to what the "to-be" architecture is to accomplish

5. "To-be" architecture "roadmap"

Enabling technologies

Provides "framework" for content and timing of specific actions and

Measure results

Ongoing year-to-year actions to achieve goals

Restructured business processes

Technology and information systems projects

Capital investments

Skill development and training

combines knowledge and understanding of today's business, corporate goals and directions, with enabling technologies, and gives us the freedom to choose different approaches to achieving tomorrow's business goal. It is the vehicle for identifying the issues and opportunities related to managing today's business and for allowing us to establish future business objectives.

System architecture, once developed, becomes the road map to the future. It provides the framework for sound judgment in the development of capital, human, and technical resources, and for the achievement of a more profitable and competitive enterprise.

# PART THREE

# Strategies for Making Business Technology Work

Deliberating on what must be done is not sufficient to begin making computer technology a critical job for achieving business goals. We must act now to prepare effectively for managing the future. Repositioning and redirecting the business technology organization is certainly one of the first steps, yet by itself it is not enough. For a truly productive environment of the future, attitudes must change. In most companies, this change in attitude begins at the uppermost levels and works its way throughout the corporate culture, from senior management to business technology management and on to the user organizations.

# 8

╥╥╥╥╥╥╥╥╥╥╥╥╥╥╥╥╥╥╥╥╥╥╥╥╥╥╥╥╥╥╥╥╥╥╥╥

# Solving Today's Problems and Building Tomorrow's Environment

Future architectures and their implementation can bring images of creativity, challenge, and fun to mind. They energize us, divert us from today's problems, and move us to exploration. Unabated, they become our sole vision of success, our sole quest. However, the real world within the walls of the business technology department must successfully support today's business with today's computer systems. Only then can we begin the transition to tomorrow's architectures. Of necessity, business technology has to deal with two quests—solving today's problems and building tomorrow's environment.

The embattled fortress was not accidental. We created it, and we did it with today's systems, today's management practices, and today's methods of delivering business technology services. But waiting for tomorrow's architectures to be put in place before we begin to remove some of the fortress walls is simply not appropriate. We must give equal concentration to both the current and the future aspects of our environment. Without improved performance in delivering our services now, we may not have the opportunity to build tomorrow's systems.

One of my company's services is turnaround management for ailing business technology departments. On these turnaround management engagements, we look at two aspects of the department:

- Business technology's performance on an everyday basis. We evaluate items such as on-line system performance, computer up time, delivery of output accurately and on time, responsiveness to the user for system modification, and delivery of systems development commitments on time.
- Whether the computer applications effectively support the business, and if they can continue to support the business in the future.

Usually we find problems in both areas; however, we approach each area individually with two separate teams. One team concentrates on today's problems, the other on tomorrow's needs. No matter how important tomorrow's systems are, today's problems will block us from achieving them if not resolved.

## A Business Within a Business

The business technology department is a business within a business. Unless it organizes and conducts itself as a business, it cannot be effective. Like any business enterprise it has customers (the users of computer technology) and it sells products (computer-based systems and services).

Each business is of course unique, and the location of business technology, whether at the corporate or division level, can only be determined by each company. But common to all companies is the necessity for the business technology department to recognize what its business is and why it is in business. It has no existence separate and apart from the business it is supporting. The business technology department should not be the controller of the computer, but rather the provider of computer technology leadership and computer services; executive management is the controller.

The two major aspects of business technology's business are that of an engineering–manufacturing company and a utility. The utility aspect is similar to that of an electric utility.

Rather than electric power, it is the supplier of computer cycles in a nondispersed environment. Like an electric utility, it must anticipate peak load requirements and be concerned about the best methods for distributing or making available those cycles to end users.

The development of computer applications that are major products produced by business technology is similar to the development of products by an engineering–manufacturing firm. If we consider the similarity between these different businesses, maybe we can begin to borrow ideas, organization structures, and practices, rather than developing our own. Consider the following comparisons:

| *Engineering/Manufacturing* | *Business Technology* |
| --- | --- |
| Research & development | System architecture planning |
| Engineering | Systems design |
| Manufacturing | Programming |
| Quality control | Quality assurance |
| Product support | Application maintenance |

The pattern suggested here is that business technology product development requirements are virtually the same as an engineering–manufacturing firm. Yet how many business technology departments have a separate quality assurance organization or a separate applications maintenance organization? In fact, in most business technology departments all of the functions identified above, if performed, are usually done by the same people. There is ample justification to consider reevaluating our approach to planning, organizing, and managing.

*Concentration on Mission.* If business technology is to become an effective contribution center for an enterprise, it must define its mission, and determine authority and responsibility. Of the three, the mission is the most critical. Responsibility and authority are only the means to achieve the mission. As I mentioned earlier in the chapter, there are two quests—solving today's problems and building tomorrow's environment, and each quest needs clear mission statements. All too often when they are combined into one, clarity of mission is lost, followed by ineffective support for either.

The present mission should direct its energies to addressing the daily activities required to support the "today" needs of the business. These activities should encompass the maintenance and enhancement of existing systems, and delivery of computer output, in an effective manner. The mission statement should focus on daily quality and delivery performance. Issues such as levels of service, computer and network availability, responsiveness to users in the modification and enhancement of systems, and response time of on-line systems should be addressed. In other words, perform today's activities at the highest quality level possible.

The future mission should address anything that creates significant change in the use of technology or the manner in which business will employ technology to meet its future objectives. The future mission requires a clearly defined and agreed-upon architecture or set of objectives as an umbrella for the mission statement.

*Organizing to Achieve the Mission.* Once business technology defines its mission, then it organizes itself for the overall mission. However, before this organization can be accomplished, consider this.

As was mentioned earlier, the organization structures that exist in most business technology departments today have not appreciably changed since the early 1960s. They were designed to support a different era in delivering computer-based services. If we are to be successful in the future, we must let go of the past and begin to define new structures, responsibilities, and delivery mechanisms that will support today's and tomorrow's demands for computer services. In essence, we must dismantle our existing business technology departments and re-form them in a more productive way to meet tomorrow's challenge.

Organizing to achieve the mission starts at the highest organizational level with the business technology department and filters down through every aspect of the organization. Management must commit itself to splitting those activities required to support today's sytems from those required to support tomorrow's systems, as Figure 5 illustrates.

Today's systems represent all existing production computer applications and their corresponding support mechanisms. Tomorrow's systems represent all activities required to achieve future or new computer applications or capabilities. But once applications or capabilities move out of the development phase into production, they then become the responsibility of today's systems. In essence, today's systems are constantly changing because they are becoming tomorrow's environment. When new applications are transferred, the staff involved in that development of the application or capability are also transferred to the today system organization. They become part of the team to support the maintenance and enhancement of that particular system. In addition, as the old computer applications or capabilities are discontinued, the staff maintaining these systems can be transferred to the tomorrow systems group to work on new development.

The important thing to remember here is the splitting of two very dissimilar activities: the engineering and manufacturing of new products and the delivery, maintenance, and support of existing products. The missions are entirely different, and they require different skills to manage, lead, and perform the activities.

## Today's Systems Organization

The responsibility of the systems organization is to deliver (on a *daily* basis) the highest-level support to the user regarding existing computer applications or services. These include quality assurance; meeting delivery commitments; and responding to daily changes within the business environment.

The focus here is supporting daily or near-term requirements of the existing business. The organization is reactive rather than proactive. It is oriented more toward discipline and responsiveness, rather than abstract creativity. Its management style is more operations- or foreman-oriented, in which service and delivery are critical. The today systems organization (the

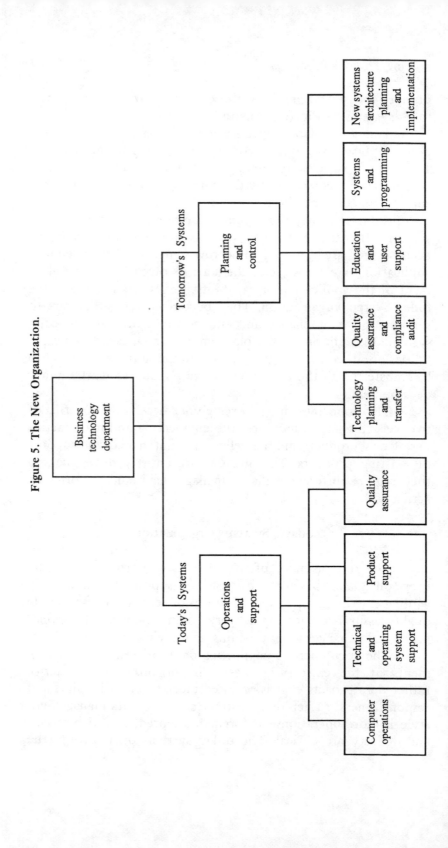

Figure 5. The New Organization.

left branch of Figure 5) is responsible for basic functions, computer operations, technical and operating systems support, product support, and quality assurance.

*Computer Operations.* The basic responsibilities of computer operations are the following:

- Deliver to the users the output of its application processing, on time and with consistent quality.
- Ensure a high level of computer system and communications network availability through proper monitoring of performance, timely resolution of problems, and proper maintenance of computer and communications hardware.
- Monitor and tune daily on-line systems networks.
- Implement adequate recovery systems in the event systems malfunction or disaster occurs.
- Maintain an operations improvement program on an ongoing basis.
- Respond to user inquiries and problems in a positive and timely manner.

*Technical and Operating Systems Support.* This function primarily addresses the technical and systems software aspects of computer operations. Its responsibilities are as follows:

- Research, modify, and update the technical quality of computer operations.
- Monitor computer and communications network performance, ensuring continuous maintenance and monitoring for optimum performance.
- Plan computer capacity for future computer systems and networks, based on the firm's goals and growth needs.

*Product Support.* The product support function addresses what has been traditionally termed as applications systems maintenance and enhancement. However, the term *product support* implies and requires a new approach to serving the user community. In the past, we have relegated this activity to the lowest priority in the department. Most corporations rely heavily on computer systems in the operation of their daily business. These systems require maintenance and enhancement in order to keep pace with changes occurring in the business, so we can no longer tolerate product support as a low priority. If we want to achieve success, product support should be one of the strongest functions within the business technology department. Its responsibilities are these:

• Maintain and enhance all major applications in production (the tomorrow systems organization is responsible for major enhancements or rewrites).
• Establish an active relationship with the user community, determining any weaknesses in the application structure, and implement modifications to increase system performance.
• Identify weaknesses in user training, and implement corrective action.
• Establish performance standards for product support delivery, and measure the organization against these standards. This includes turnaround time for a user service request, problem solving, answering an inquiry, and tracking the percentage of product enhancement delivery commitment dates that are met.

*Quality Assurance.* As its name implies, this function maintains high standards and quality for all system products and services. Very few business technology departments have a quality assurance (QA) function, or if they do, they only pay it lip service. This is one of the major reasons for the computer industry's sloppy performance. Yet as business relies more and more on computer technology, lack of QA greatly increases the risk of errors or failure. Responsibilities of QA include these:

• Develop appropriate standards, operating practices and procedures, application maintenance procedures, change control practices, and so forth.
• Manage production systems, change control, and testing activities.

- Develop, monitor, and prepare service-level performance reporting, based on agreements with user organizations.
- Develop, monitor, and maintain effective control, security, file backup/retention, and disaster/recovery systems.

If we are going to improve today's business technology delivery systems, it is imperative that a separate organization be placed in charge of them. Assign a high priority to this activity, staff it with dedicated professionals who understand their mission, and you will see a threefold improvement in system performance within one year. If you choose not to, consider this: All your "tomorrow systems" will simply be "today systems," running in the same operating environment as last year and the year before, increasing the daily work load, and moving toward the day when they ultimately crash, seriously impairing your business operations.

### The Tomorrow Systems Organization

This organization's mission is to guide, manage, and orchestrate the design, development, and implementation of the computer systems and capabilities needed to achieve the firm's future business goals. It is in charge of the architecture of tomorrow described in Chapter Six.

The words *guide, manage,* and *orchestrate* are critical in this context. If it is a dispersed architecture, some of the design development and implementation may be performed at the departmental level. In this case, *guide* or *orchestrate* may refer to the form of leadership. Where the tomorrow systems organization is performing the work itself, the word *manage* also applies.

The tomorrow systems organization (the right branch of Figure 5) is planning- and project-oriented, rather than operationally oriented like the today systems organization. The management style is more creative, more business-oriented, and works on timely and efficient project delivery.

The right branch of Figure 5 identifies the various functions that need to be put in place to support tomorrow's architecture. This is a project-driven organization and should be designed to work like an accordion, expanding and contracting in accordance with the number of projects and the staff required for them. This could be as few as half a dozen or as many as several hundred staff members at any given time. The future architecture design and the plan for migrating to it help determine the size of the organization and the types of groups comprising it.

Such an organization is not built overnight. In the beginning, it may be a single planning entity, such as the skunk works team detailed in Chapter Seven. This is obviously the place to begin; any new endeavor requires planning and direction. Gradually, you build and expand the organization, group by group, adding people as necessary. Because the number of people in each suborganization will expand or contract depending on the number of projects being worked on, outside contractors should be considered for supporting peak staffing requirements.

The theory of having a separate tomorrow organization applies whether you have the whole of a new architecture plan or several major projects to be developed. Future projects should be established outside the mainstream of the everyday support activities of business technology. Otherwise, you will have conflict of missions and both the new projects and support of the daily business activities will suffer.

The tomorrow systems organization has responsibility for five functions: new systems architecture planning and implementation; technology planning and transfer; systems and programming; education and user support; and quality assurance and compliance audit.

*New Systems Architecture Planning and Implementation.* This group should be comprised of seasoned business personnel and business-oriented technologists. The mix is critical to ensure systems that are business-driven, not technology-driven. In addition, when this group develops a system for a particular business function, its staff should be involved in the requirements, design, implementation, and project management. The responsibilities are these:

• Work with the business organization to plan future systems, develop appropriate system architectures, prepare migration plans, and manage the transition from today's to tomorrow's systems that provides greater benefits to the business.

• Work with users and the systems and programming group to define the detailed requirements for new computer applications or capabilities, based on the new architecture. If a user department or function is developing its own requirements, this group reviews, suggests modifications, and approves them.

• Use matrix management to oversee all the projects being designed, developed, and implemented by the tomorrow systems organization and guide their implementation.

• Counsel with senior management on future systems, act as liaison for current projects, and help determine project funding approvals.

*Technology Planning and Transfer.* This group addresses the more technical, rather than managerial, aspects of future architecture planning. Its responsibilities are as follows:

• Keep abreast of current and emerging technology developments in computer hardware, software, communications systems, office automation, robotics, artificial intelligence, and so forth, and perform research and development to determine the use and applicability of these technologies.

• Work with the new systems architecture planning and implementation group to determine appropriate technology to achieve the firm's goals and mission.

• Establish and enforce technical guidelines and standards for compatibility between various technologies and components in the system architecture.

• Manage the new technology implementation.

• Transfer new technology to other organizations within the business.

*Systems and Programming.* This group actually oversees and performs the detailed design, programming, testing, and implementation of applications for the new systems architecture.

*Education and User Support.* This is crucial in moving toward the new systems architecture. It is the central source for disseminating information on the technology, standards, policies, practices, and management responsibilities. Many companies are moving into new computer systems; some of them are even dispersing computer power. However, all too often this is happening in an unplanned, unstructured manner, with little or no training.

Put simply, we cannot afford to allow each user to learn by his or her own mistakes. Untold millions of dollars are wasted every year because first-time personal computer users had no prior training. If users have the right to acquire their own computer systems—and I believe in many cases they have that right —then management and the business technology staff share the responsibility to help them gain the knowledge to ensure their proficiency.

There is a body of knowledge available on how to manage computer resources, how to use hardware and software, how to protect an organization from data security breaches, malfunctions, and disasters, and how to achieve effective system design and implementation. This information should be available to user organizations, but more importantly, this group should provide the education, the training, and the ongoing support necessary to sustain efficient computer usage. As organizations choose to acquire and install their own computer systems, *education should be mandatory.* The education and user support group's responsibilities are as follows:

• Educate and train users in all aspects of computer systems, from selection through implementation, including standards, practices, protocol, backup and recovery, security, and so forth.

• Act as a consulting group to user organizations, either providing the support and assistance to help users acquire their own computer systems or appointing a competent outside consultant to do so.

*Quality Assurance and Compliance Audit.* There is no substitute for paying attention to quality, whether it is in the today or the tomorrow systems organization. It ensures stable, error-free computing. The difference is that the today organization imposes quality on existing systems, whereas the tomorrow organization builds it into new systems. Responsibilities are:

• Develop, or cause to be developed, standards, procedures, systems development and project management methodologies, and management practices, and assure company-wide compliance. Annual compliance audits of user organizations are essential.
• Review all major projects within the business technology organization at prescribed intervals to assure accuracy and compliance with established standards and practices.
• Administer system acceptance tests for all new business technology–developed systems.

Our experience has borne out how successful a tomorrow systems organization can be. By breaking the organization into these five functional groups, they form a composite team, each with its own goals, but together committed to excellence at creating and implementing tomorrow systems. And of course, once the tomorrow systems are in place, they are turned over to the today systems organization, who apply their own expertise.

## Building Tomorrow's Environment

At the beginning of the chapter, I said it may be difficult to create this new business technology department. There will be internal resistance over the means and methods employed, not only in business technology but in the user community. Your guiding vision should be these two facts: First, the business technology department must change its basic structure and methods of delivering services to meet the changing needs of the firm. Second, separating its activities into the today systems and the tomorrow systems organizations is the first step in changing its performance, attitude, and working environment.

## Cost and Other Issues

These are some of the arguments that will be brought forward to the person or persons contemplating change:

- What will it cost?
- All our good people are on maintenance.
- If we make radical changes, Charlie will leave.

*What Will It Cost?* First, the business executives are in control of what is important to the corporation and where the monies should be expended; therefore, decisions concerning the scope of the migration effort and at what pace the migration should proceed is ultimately theirs.

Second, as was pointed out in Chapter Six, money is continuing to be spent on computers and computer systems at an increasing rate, and the delta cost to split the organization and do it right is very little, if any. It is a matter of redistribution of resources.

Third, you may have noticed when presenting the above organization synopsis I chose to use the word *function* rather than *organization* entity. The reason for this is that a structure is highly dependent on organization size. Small organizations may choose to collapse several functions into one organization entity. The important thing here is that each function exist in some manner, but not necessarily as a separate organization.

*All Our Good People Are on Maintenance.* These are the people needed to develop the new systems, but it will be asserted that they are the only people on staff who are good enough to maintain existing systems. Another argument is that if business technology professionals are put into a maintenance or product support organization, they will leave. This is not a people problem, it is a management problem. First of all, maintaining existing systems requires top-notch capability. If those are the only good people in your organization, that is a problem. You do not have a balanced organization. The argument of people leaving is also not valid. I have been involved with organizations that have established a product support group and the programmers and analysts did not leave. It is an important function and can be an exciting function as well, if carefully established and explained.

One additional point that I believe we often overlook is that it takes different human characteristics to do R&D, systems design and programming of large systems, and product support. This does not mean that one person's capabilities are better than another's. It is just that these are different types of jobs, any one of which an individual may perform more effectively. Within an engineering–manufacturing company you will normally find these groupings of engineers: R&D engineers, design engineers, and product support engineers. Each function requires a high degree of engineering skill, but the application of these skills is dramatically different.

*If We Make Radical Changes, Charlie Will Leave.* There is always the probability that Charlie will leave. If he is so important to the organization that it will collapse without him, then again you have a management problem. If Charlie is the block in developing a better organization, then I question the true value of Charlie related to the organization. I am not being callous. I believe the Charlies of the world are important and should be treated as such. Ample consideration should be given to them in developing a new organization. However, if it's not to their liking, give them the right to make the decision on their own behalf.

And one final point is the issue of splitting the organization. It creates significant visibility into the business technology department from a budgeting and funding standpoint. The today systems organization can be compared to a zero-base budget. Those expenditures are necessary to maintain your current business. The tomorrow systems organization involves discretionary budgeting. This creates clarity for the business executive to choose the route to take in using technology to support the business in the future, and the monies to spend year by year. It also gives the business technology department executive clarity to guide the business being supported with the technology of the future. It is that clarity that forms a partnership.

# 9

⊓⊔⊓⊔⊓⊔⊓⊔⊓⊔⊓⊔⊓⊔⊓⊔⊓⊔⊓⊔⊓⊔⊓⊔⊓⊔⊓⊔⊓⊔⊓⊔⊓⊔⊓⊔

# Developing New Methods of Control for Business Technology

Moving from the old, centralized computer architecture to the new, dispersed architecture means moving from the complex to the simple. And this encourages clarity, which presents opportunities for finding new and better ways of doing things.

The dispersed architecture demands that we find new ways to address the issue of control. Once computing is dispersed, the old, centralized methods will not work any longer. We must discover new ways of thinking about hardware, software, and how we manage the computer resource. Machiavelli wrote:

> There is nothing more difficult to take in hand, more perilous to conduct, or more uncertain in its success, than to take the lead in the introduction of the new order of things.

But that is exactly what we must do, for we are creating and managing the future of the business.

Dispersed computing is the devolution of responsibility to the lowest effective level. However, this devolution does not eliminate the need for a central management responsibility to guide, balance, and implement a dispersed architecture. The architecture described previously requires a company-wide infrastructure and a set of standards to ensure communications and data compatibility between functions and organizations. I know of otherwise well-managed companies that, in their zeal to decentralize computing, have lost control of their integrated computer applications. Why? Because from a business standpoint they lost the ability to see how the various pieces were supposed to work together.

Two things must be in place prior to moving into dispersed computing. First, an overall system architecture must exist to guide, model, and influence the implementation; and second, a business technology organization must exist, with central management responsibility and authority to oversee it. Without these two elements, the likelihood of a successful dispersal is slim.

Dispersed computing is going to happen; in fact, it is happening now. The first wave of dispersed computing was the proliferation of personal computers; the second wave is the move toward departmental computing, which began in 1985. The continued movement toward smaller, cheaper, and more powerful computers and more user-friendly software will surely cause another wave of dispersed computing.

Old control techniques will not stem the tide. Creative control is the answer in the management of dispersal, so that it does not occur willy-nilly, as is often the case. It is much easier to develop and implement control structures before things get under way than it is to straighten them out after the fact.

## Understanding Control

What is control? There are many definitions. Good control observes current performance, in people or in systems, and guides it toward the firm's goals. Control is the outgrowth of the planning process, the means by which we guide events toward a desired outcome. It is wise observation; it is caring about how things are done; it is paying close attention to details. Most important, perhaps, it is a positive "yes" attitude, a desire to find ways to achieve goals.

What is creative control? It is giving people the tools they need to do their work properly and productively, then giving them the space in which to do it. Creative control does not require checkpoints, but it does measure results. Under yesterday's centralized business technology organization, control was exercised by limiting access to the computer or by restricting its functionality to specific users, or even by not responding to requests. In a dispersed environment, the central business technology organization does not have this kind of control. Its mission is simply to ensure that users are able to select, develop, and operate computer systems with reasonable skill within the company's overall system architectural objectives. Beyond that, business technology exercises no control at all; what the users do with the computer is strictly their own business.

Robert Umbaugh, an executive at Southern California Edison, put it this way: "The goal has to be to make sure that the computer is not an exception, that it is a normal part of the process. As long as we consider it an exception, it will get undue attention" (interview, May 21, 1985). Creative control gives us the ability to make computers a normal part of the business, so long as we have a strategy that supports sustained, ongoing dispersal.

## The Creative Control Hierarchy

Creative control must be exercised at all three levels of the dispersed computing environment: the enterprise level, the departmental level, and the ad hoc level. Naturally, it begins with senior management's commitment and approval; it must be made clear throughout the organization that along with the new dispersed computer architecture, control is being refocused and dispersed as well.

*The Enterprise Level.* It is here that senior management's wishes are implemented—in other words, from where planning and control are exercised throughout the company. Controls are tightest at this level. The restructured centralized business technology organization still has a mission and must support the entire firm's common needs. This central function is constantly working on and guiding the dispersal of the new architecture throughout the company.

*The Departmental Level.* Here, divisional or departmental managers have control of their own computing resources, and address their own needs for maintenance, new application development, and so forth. Their responsibility is to follow the overall company-wide guidelines, rules, and decision processes established at the enterprise level and that are set down by the business technology department. The goal here is to ensure that the data leaving their departments meet company integrity standards.

*The Ad Hoc Level.* This is where we find the users, so controls are loosest at this level, and innovation is highest. These users must adhere to the business technology standards, but those standards must already be in place at the departmental level. Ideally, the business technology department trains these users, which helps maintain the standards and guidelines.

Here is how one company we worked with described their plan for creative control. They term the enterprise level *planning and control* and departmental, *divisional,* but the functions are the same.

> In order to achieve the objective of the system architecture and to correlate the elements of this architecture to business plans, the Planning and Control function will be responsible for these activities:
>
> - Developing and coordinating plans to implement the system architecture in terms of overall business objectives
> - Providing individual department guidelines for system planning activities to support architectural requirements
> - Prioritization of architectural-related projects and concurrence with user organizations' supporting plans and schedules

- Planning for and multi-year allocation of resources to implement the system architecture
  with respect to funding sources, including internal systems development overhead budget ap-
  propriation; customer funded factory modern-
  ization contracts; and product-related budget
  appropriations.

### Developing Division Level Systems

The initial emphasis will be to further develop the implementation plan for the architecture.
Planning and Control will define implementation
steps for division level systems and identify need
dates for affected department level systems. Planning and Control will act as a Program Office and
obtain costs and time estimates from applicable organizations. These estimates will be integrated into
an overall division automation plan by Planning
and Control. . . . In this manner, the Planning and
Control function acts as a contractor and is ultimately responsible for the success of the architecture to support division level objectives. . . . A
major objective is to remove the complexities from
the large centralized systems.

### Developing Ad Hoc Applications

Department management will be responsible
for funding ad hoc applications development. Ad
hoc applications may include analysis of existing
data bases using general-purpose software, stand-
alone self-contained applications for individual
users, etc. Planning and Control will be responsible
for establishing standards and preferred sources for
such applications, e.g., programming languages,
back-up, etc. Access to departmental level data
bases will be controlled by the department responsible for the data base. Such access will not be un-
reasonably withheld.

As you can see, this report upholds the spirit and the letter of the new dispersed architecture in this company. There is no disgruntledness or animosity in this document.

## Establishing Creative Control

The way creative control techniques are applied varies from company to company. You must find the ones best suited to your needs and corporate culture. However, there are a number of points that, in our experience, routinely need to be addressed.

*Business Technology's New Role.* At the enterprise level the business technology department is in charge of planning and executing the new dispersed architecture. However, that does not extend to making the purchase decisions or telling users how they should or should not use the technology. Robert Umbaugh, whom I quoted earlier, said it this way: "It is not data processing's responsibility to control how a worker uses his desk, his calculator, or his telephone. Why the computer? If anyone assumes this responsibility, it should be the worker's supervisor, for it's his job to make sure the resources are used efficiently."

Any form of control at this level should be limited to assuring that the business functions stay within the architectural framework. It's not to control "computer proliferation," or to control legitimate access to the data base. The purpose of control is not to say no to people, but to say yes. Control is to make certain no user or organization is trying to establish their own computer hegemony. The object of control is to make sure that computing power is being properly dispersed—moved into the hands of those who need it. Business technology should be instrumental in helping users understand their role in the dispersed architecture, and should actively support new concepts and ideas with executive management.

*The User Organization's New Role.* Along with the dispersal of computers outward into the user organizations (and, in many cases, the dispersal of system development) comes the dispersal of accountability. The users can no longer blame their failures on business technology. Responsibility and accountability for performance have shifted to the users. This is not a point to be taken lightly, for I have seen too many cases where the user organization's management has created failures due to their unwillingness to take the time to understand the true scope of a system project or to devote adequate resources to its completion. The success of dispersed computing will come from the willingness of the user organization and its management to become involved, not delegating it to a hired technical hand and walking away. That is the old way of thinking. As the English poet and satirist Hilaire Belloc wrote: "But scientists, who ought to know/Assure us that it must be so./Oh, let us never, never doubt/What nobody is sure about." For dispersed computing to be effective, the responsible user management must become educated in the use, control, and delivery of computer technology within their individual organizations. They must gain an understanding of the overall corporate system architecture, and respect the need for company-wide technical leadership and standards for achieving effective dispersed computing.

*Information System Costs.* When information systems were isolated from the other organizations, they were considered a capital cost, like plant and equipment. But under the dispersed architecture, when computers are moved into user organizations, they become a cost of doing business; therefore, cost is no longer the issue. The business technology director does not need to know what the firm's computer costs are any longer. Approval procedures change. All computers—not just personal computers—become an expendable resource. When an organization outgrows a computer system, it is offered to another organization that is preparing to become dispersed. Under creative control, the issues more important than cost are value received and productivity returns.

*Setting Standards.* The old business technology department always advocated standards, even though sometimes it merely paid lip service to them. Standards are important in a dispersed architecture in the same way that a corporate accounting manual is important for the firm's departmental controllers. There are hundreds of computer hardware vendors, dozens of operating systems, many approaches to communications networks, and a thousand other variables that must be reckoned with if the various components in a computer system are to be compatible with one another. If we are to ensure communications and data compatibility between units, then technical standards are mandatory. There can be few exceptions if the dispersed architecture is going to work.

But let's approach this cautiously. Not every computer your company uses requires system integration, and if it does not, the same standards need not apply. For example, if the firm has standardized on IBM PC–compatible personal computers but a user wants a Macintosh, that is acceptable so long as the user is aware of incompatibility problems. The business technology department may not support the Macintosh, and the user must accept that fact. However, this isn't sufficient cause to disapprove the acquisition. If it effectively supports the user's needs, the computer should be acquired.

Before moving toward a dispersed environment, standards and practices should also exist for systems development, project management, documentation, security, data dictionaries, and computer operations. In developing these standards and practices, one must continually remember that a dispersed environment is considerably different than centralized environments and will require new thinking. There must be a balance between too much structure and not enough structure. To impose centralized business technology methodologies arbitrarily on the user community simply will not work. Separate sets of standards should be developed for each type of computer usage. Complex or important company-wide computer applications should have a separate set of standards and practices, as opposed to applications that are more individually oriented. The point here is balance and simplicity. If standards are impractical or too costly, they will not be accepted and, therefore, are unenforceable.

*Education.* People must learn the proper way to use technology as an enabling device, and the business technology department should be responsible for user education. Everyone in the company must be educated in the new ways and methods. Because business technology is in charge of standards and implementation, they are in an ideal position to provide the training and education as well.

Everyone who uses a computer of any size or shape should be required to take a course in computers from business technology. A curriculum might range from a basic introductory course to others covering telecommunications, operating systems, specific applications, and how to use off-the-shelf personal computer software packages. All users, including management, regardless of prior experience, should be certified by business technology before they can use a computer in the dispersed environment. There should be an open door to the education program so that anyone can come back for refresher courses or further education at any time. Managers should be required to take the certification course prior to choosing equipment for their departments, as the course will be invaluable in helping them make better buying decisions.

Interestingly, education, when properly implemented, can take the place of some of the old control systems. In a centralized architecture, what was then information systems claimed it had to have control over the computers because the users did not understand the computer and would foul things up. Under a dispersed architecture, users are taught how *not* to foul things up.

And furthermore, business technology, by assuming responsibility for education, could actually end up an even greater and more powerful force in the corporation. This approach creates control through knowledge. The kind of power information systems had in the past was power by control—simple "no" power or veto power, a false power that, like a dictator's, can be lost at any time. But teaching people is a leadership activity, and it bestows true power in that the teacher imparts knowledge and influences the students, giving them something they didn't have before. Teaching truly is a leadership activity, with all the freedom and responsibilities—and power—that suggests.

*Stewardship.* Business technology must become the users' steward, the people and place the users turn to when they need information, help, tips, techniques, or even a forum for sharing ideas about getting the most from their computers. If information systems lost its role as innovator years ago, this is where it all comes back, for now business technology is freed from the awesome responsibilities for all the company's computer resources. They can share ideas with users in an unencumbered environment.

Business technology, in this stewardship role, must also be conscious of their responsibility to the business as a whole. They must ensure that computer systems operating throughout the business are performing within acceptable standards. Here, periodic reviews or audits are necessary to fulfill the stewardship role.

The critical thing to understand about the review in a dispersed environment is what its limits should be. The review should not evaluate the appropriateness of the applications operating on a dispersed computer. That decision is the prerogative of the user department. But rather, review should focus on the effectiveness of the operating environment in which the applications are operating. Compliance with company-wide business technology standards and operating practices is the key ingredient. Elements of the review may include items such as the decision process in use for choosing applications, acceptable levels of documentation, appropriate security, back-up procedures, operating procedures, and so forth.

The review should be accomplished as a value-added service within the dispersed computing environment. In other words, the organization being reviewed should benefit over the long term in having a high-performance operating environment.

The implementation of a system of control relating to these points will be a major step forward along the new path in developing a strong business technology organization. As the embattled fortress crumbles, and all the old control issues disappear, what emerges is business technology's true power to lead and influence users. It will help them reach their organization's productivity goals and thus the firm's goals, rather than hindering them as has happened in the past.

## Freedom and Responsibility

The key to creative control is understanding that it has two elements: freedom and responsibility. Both must be used wisely. Business technology must begin to trust and respect the users. The user must begin to accept that business technology has a rightful and important role in bringing about and monitoring technology change within the business.

Nowhere are freedom and responsibility more important than in training and education. Business technology must learn the freedom to share what it knows without fear of loss or diminishment. The responsibility is heavy, for the entire company is depending on business technology to lead the way into the future. Business technology's degree of commitment to the dispersed architecture will be evident in the way they handle this responsibility.

Every organization is different. Therefore, it is up to you to act with foresight in establishing the appropriate creative control techniques for your business. When it's done right, creative control appears to be no control at all.

# 10

````
ЛTГLTГLTГLTГLTГLTГLTГLTГLTГLTГLTГLTГLTГLTГLTГLTГЛ
````

## Executive Involvement: Aligning Business Technology and Company Objectives

John F. Kennedy, speaking in a televised address on Independence Day, 1960, said:

> It is a time for a new generation of leadership, to
> cope with new problems and new opportunities.
> For there is a new world to be won.

This is certainly true of the effort to lead the firm into the effective use of computer technology. We have encountered many executives who despair of trying to deal with the business technology department and, for all intents and purposes, have given up. Yet in our work we have seen many executives quickly learn enough to make the right decisions about business technology by building the proper framework with which to understand and manage the department. They are, to paraphrase President Kennedy, the new generation of leaders. It is essential that the business technology department get this executive leadership. But why, you may ask, is this function singled out for special attention, above and beyond the normal business management patterns?

129

The answer lies in the value of the computer as one of the key business performance tools of the future. It can also be a strategic and competitive weapon for many businesses as well. Failure to marry the business technology directions with business objectives can be costly and perhaps disastrous.

It is no secret that in many companies the executive body is highly dissatisfied with the performance of the business technology organization. Business technology, on the other hand, often wishes to meet with the executives because they realize the direction in which they are going is no longer supporting the company's direction, and they want to resolve the issue. But when they request this meeting, more often than not the answer they receive is, We don't have time to deal with this issue. Anyway, your organization should know what to do. Just deliver what the user organizations ask for. One such company is spending about $20 million on new systems that will not support the future direction of the company. Yet a one-day meeting with the executive body could redirect this expenditure for the long-term benefit of the company, with minimal impact on its short-term goals.

Working with more than one hundred companies over the past fifteen years has convinced me beyond any doubt that those companies with significant and continuing executive involvement had high-performing business technology departments. Those that didn't, regardless of how effective their business technology executive was as a leader, ended up with inefficient, poorly performing departments.

There are four critical reasons for continuing executive involvement. First, because of the rapid rate of change in computer technology since the beginning of the 1980s, there are many new products and services available that require close scrutiny. Second, with the changes in technology and the general economic climate, it has become imperative that business technology dollars be spent wisely to aid the company in achieving its goals and mission. Third, computers have infiltrated every aspect of the business; therefore, decisions concerning business technology have a direct impact on the firm and every organization within it. And fourth, this proliferation has caused demand for computer services to far outstrip business technology's resources, necessitating senior management's active participation in planning for current and future service demands.

Decisions like this should not be left solely in the hands of business technology executives. They normally do not have sufficient knowledge about the business and its directions to make the appropriate decisions. Nor should decisions be delegated to a "user committee" that can only achieve, at best, watered-down compromises that provide little or no benefit to the business. Decisions about computer technology should be made at two different levels in the firm: at the executive level by a board of business executives, and then in business technology. There are three aspects to the process: first, the executive must gain control; second, a business technology executive policy committee must be established; and third, clear management policies must be developed for the three levels of the dispersed architecture.

### Executive Control

Executive control of business technology systems should increase visibility and understanding of various computer technology systems, so that through timely and concise guidance, the executive can bring better decisions to bear upon improving the company's operational performance. To achieve this, I feel it is essential that executive management involve itself directly in managing and directing business technology. Business technology's mission must come from goals and objectives established by executive management.

This fact was brought home to the chief operating officer at one of our Fortune 500 clients, who had hired us to reposition the business technology department. Early in the engagement, I encouraged him to establish and head a business technology executive policy committee, made up of the key executives reporting to him. As discussions ensued, he finally told me he didn't think such a committee was necessary, that he and his executives were busy and didn't have the time to concern themselves with how the computer technology was deployed. "Jim,"

I replied, "I understand and respect your position, and agree with you. We in the business technology department know what systems need to be implemented to increase the company's efficiency, and are fully capable of making those decisions for you. Thank you for your confidence. We appreciate it." He sat back and thought about what I'd said; then we began to discuss the formation of a committee.

### The Business Technology Executive Policy Committee

The business technology executive cannot lead business technology alone. For that reason, I recommend a business technology executive policy committee that embodies the interests of senior management and the various functions they represent. The committee orchestrates the diverse interests and needs of the entire company into one business technology policy and practice. In some firms it may be called the steering committee or steering board, but in any case, its responsibility is to assess, monitor, and make policy regarding business technology budgets and operations. These responsibilities include:

- Setting business technology objectives and strategies
- Defining operational policies
- Appointing top business technology executives
- Approving the business technology organizational structure
- Assuring business technology plans are in balance with the company's long-range goals
- Reviewing budgets and approving major expenditures
- Approving and monitoring application development projects
- Monitoring business technology's responsiveness to all services performed
- Representing business technology to the rest of the company

The business technology executive policy committee should mirror the corporation's board of directors in its thinking and practices, with its sole purpose defining and guiding business technology's activities. The committee orchestrates the diverse interests and needs of the whole company into harmonious practice, and it chooses the menu of tactics to execute the strategy. The emphasis is on service and delivery expectations. The committee coalesces all these forces into a coherent and workable business technology operating philosophy that is in perfect synchronization with the firm's needs and goals.

Carrying the analogy further, there are several other ways the business technology executive policy committee is like a board of directors. Both the board and the committee mandate policies and practices designed to meet prescribed goals. They disseminate this information, along with details on committee membership, operation rules, and information requirements, to the company at large.

When a company plans a new building or expansion, the board is briefed; such is the case when business technology proposes additional computer technology. We encourage a proposal called a "decision package" that communicates in business terminology, not computer jargon, just exactly what the system will do for the user or the company.

Just as a board gets quarterly reports on earnings and the company's general health, so the committee receives reports on business technology's pulse and temperature. With our clients, its health is measured in reports such as "Problem Reports Backlog," "Two-Year Resource Projection," and "Summary of Completed Requests."

Although a single committee usually serves the small, or single-product company, larger corporations sometimes set up a multiple-committee hierarchy. Separate committees guide the business technology activities for each division, reporting in turn to a higher policy committee mindful of broader corporate goals.

Also, in a dispersed architecture, each department manager should have a similar committee governing those systems, computers, and technical resources under his or her charge. The committee membership of the division or the department in a dispersed architecture should be structured in a manner similar to the top-level committee.

*Committee Membership.* Just as a corporation's board must strive to represent the diverse interests of the corporation, the business technology executive policy committee must do the same. A successful committee includes the company president, a senior executive from various organizations and functions (such as finance, marketing, personnel, or manufacturing), and the director of business technology. Ideally, there should be more than three members, but not more than twelve. When properly established, the committee has the authority to make decisions and allocate resources; in fact, if it cannot do so, there is little point in having it.

The business technology executive policy committee usually meets monthly or every other month. Attendance is mandatory, especially during the formative period, when the committee is finding its personality and voice. Each member should have full voting authority.

*Making It Work.* There is a risk that the business technology executive policy committee could fail in its mission. Most committees run the risk of failure due to executive negligence, making its agenda a low priority, or just plain ineptitude. You cannot allow this committee to fail, for there is little likelihood a successor would have any credibility at all. Therefore, we have found the following rules, if strictly adhered to, give the committee a better-than-average chance of success:

- The committee is chaired by the president or the most senior executive
- There is only executive-level membership, and no permanent alternates
- There must be regular meetings with an established agenda
- The committee is the only body permitted to establish policies and priorities for the business technology resource
- Business technology must make all its activities, including cost and budget allocations, known to the committee
- The committee establishes priorities, policies, and implementation schedules for all computer technology throughout the company
- Decisions regarding allocation of business technology resources and monies are binding upon the entire corporation
- Committee decisions are binding throughout the company.

Several assumptions are made here. First, the committee must regard business technology as a business within a business—a company investment and not a cost center. Second, in a dispersed computing environment as outlined in this book, any user organization with its own computing power is subject to the committee's decisions in the same way the business technology department is. And third, all decisions regarding technology are submitted for committee approval using the decision package.

*The Decision Package.* The decision package is a set of documents detailing the user organization's request for additional computer resources. It allows the committee to review the nature and scope of the request in a standardized form and understandable vocabulary so the committee can make the hard choices as to how business technology dollars are spent.

Decision packages should accompany the agenda that is circulated before each committee meeting. A thoroughly prepared package describes the proposed development project, explaining its nature, cost, and benefits, and answers the following questions:

- What purpose does the project serve? Is it essential (that is, for legal or tax reasons), or is it intended to enhance current capabilities?
- What are the hard dollar and soft dollar costs and benefits? What is the cost–benefit ratio?
- Is current hardware sufficient to develop and implement the project? If not, what is needed, and what will it cost?
- Are people needed to staff the project? Are they currently available? If not, what additional staff are required? How will they be obtained, and at what cost?

Decision packages must be complete, and must adhere to stringent format and content guidelines so the committee can fairly and accurately compare competing projects. Requests for minor maintenance to existing systems need not go through this process, but can be handled by the business technology director.

The decision package ensures that only the most worthy projects will be approved, based on the committee's recommendation.

*Committee Costs and Benefits.* In addition to subjecting decision packages to a cost-benefit analysis, we can analyze the business technology executive policy committee in the same manner. The major cost is time, for the members must not only sit upon the committee, but must evaluate decision criteria in between meetings. Committee members are among the most highly paid in the firm, so their time is indeed valuable. Yet the benefits are easily and quickly measured.

In a large insurance company, this type of policy committee caused a shift in the company's perception of the business technology department. Once that department had the benefit of top management's insight into the critical business and automation issues, things began to change. The system development staff was reduced from fifty people to thirty-eight as a result of matching business technology resources to business needs. The business technology department was turned into a solid support organization for achieving company growth and productivity. Business technology turned from being poor performers into a team of outstanding performers, and executive management believes the business technology executive policy committee was the key.

The very act of forming the business technology executive policy committee announces to users and the business technology staff alike that *senior management takes business technology seriously.* No other function warrants a monthly meeting of the firm's key executives; therefore, it must be profoundly important. As a result, morale improves and productivity immediately rises. The business technology staff begins to contemplate the term *professionalism* again, and to return in kind the attention and concern shown to them. This is not witchcraft, not mesmerism, but the "Hawthorne Effect," which Elton Mayo first observed among workers at Western Electric in the late 1920s.

In another example, a manufacturing firm created an

executive policy committee that was able to implement discipline and gain control of the business technology organization for the first time in the company's history. Prior to this, no one had any confidence in the business technology organization. It was unreliable and performed poorly. Now there are both dependability and good communications, which fostered a new attitude in the company and has helped restore trust in the business technology organization. In fact, the executive policy committee's work with business technology was so successful that they are using the same approach to control the engineering R&D function.

The wise business technology director will capitalize on the committee in other ways. Using the committee's knowledge and insight, he or she can plan more certainly and aggressively, ask questions and get the right answers, and respond in ways that garner immediate approval and success. There is no longer any need to try and second-guess what the company or the individual user wants, or what priority to assign a new application request.

In the final analysis, everybody wins. The business technology executive policy committee provides the long-missing guidance that business technology needs. It has the wisdom and the perspective to allocate business technology resources appropriately, to ensure the maximum contribution to the firm's mission, and the maximum return as well. In just a few months, the committee can help transform the embattled fortress into an optimistic, productive, and professional business technology organization.

# Epilogue

꛲꛲꛲꛲꛲꛲꛲꛲꛲꛲꛲꛲꛲꛲꛲꛲꛲꛲꛲꛲꛲

# Challenging the Status Quo:
# A Samurai Strategy
# for the Future

The mission I set for myself in writing this book was to create a challenge for the thinking reader. My goal was to stimulate a quest for solutions to your firm's business technology problems. I have presented many ideas and solutions that I have personally found successful. Yet each business is different, and what has worked for others should only be considered a starting point for your own creative problem solving. Your needs, your objectives, and your business technology department are all different from any other firm's, so your goals will be different, too.

Yet within each business there is a question common to all that must be answered. Are yesterday's approaches and business technology practices viable for the future? If your answer is no, then I urge you to join the quest.

It will not be easy. The old tools, the old methods of operating, and the old ideas will be difficult to change. When you threaten an organization's culture, battle lines may be drawn. However, if we keep a clear vision and understand that culture or custom often make the unnatural appear natural and, conversely, the natural appear unnatural, then those battle lines may not be so sharply drawn.

If we are to achieve success in creating change of this magnitude, it is important to understand how to use strategy to make the way of the future. For me, the strategy to use is a samurai strategy. I have long admired the Japanese samurai as the world's noblest questers. These knights were members of an aristocratic class formed in the eighth century A.D. They practiced kendo, the Way of the sword, for over a thousand years. They were educated in the arts, literature, and the social graces while they learned swordsmanship. Where the Westerner would say, "The pen is mightier than the sword," a samurai would say, "Bunbu itchi," or "Pen and sword in accord."

One of the greatest samurai was Miyamoto Musashi (1584–1645). Between the ages of thirteen and twenty-nine, he fought more than sixty opponents and beat them all. He eventually had no need of real swords, and substituted wooden ones in their place.

One reason I feel Musashi was so formidable was that he trained his mind as well as his body. He spent his last years living in a cave, writing his thoughts down in what was to become known as *A Book of Five Rings.** Musashi himself called it "a guide for men who want to learn strategy. . . . When you have attained the Way of strategy there will be not one thing you cannot understand.

"Strategy," Musashi continues, "is the craft of the warrior." I believe that strategy is the craft of the successful quester as well. Correct strategy creates an opportunity to solve problems. Poor strategy leads to communication distortion and, often, to failure.

The manner in which we use and manage computer technology is desperately in need of some soul-searching and a new strategy. A good strategy means, first of all, understanding the problem, and second, understanding people's vested interests in their work. Unless we are willing to ask questions and challenge

*Miyamoto Musashi, *A Book of Five Rings* (Woodstock, N.Y.: The Overlook Press, 1974; tr. Victor Harris).

some basic assumptions about using computers in business today, then we won't be able to understand the problem. Once
the issues are identified, we can develop a strategy for making
the necessary changes.

The first step is to look at things on a broad scale. Widen
your vision as much as possible, for small changes in tools and
techniques will not produce the benefits we seek. Our broad-
based strategy requires that we first come to know our enemy.

The enemy is not the business technology department. It
is not the user. It is not the computer manufacturer. The enemy
is the status quo—continuing to accept yesterday's solutions to
support tomorrow's organization. We industry professionals
should have understood by this time that centralization versus
decentralization (regardless of the latest label attached to it) is
not the issue. Neither is it the business technology department's
performance, nor the difference of opinion between business
people and computer people. These are only symptoms, and obviously changes need to be made in each of these areas. But
what kind of changes? We cannot answer that question until we
understand the broader, strategic issue: How and in what manner are we going to use computer technology in the future?

## For the Business Executive

The ultimate challenge in employing technology successfully rests squarely on senior management's shoulders. Without
your support and guidance, the business technology executive
cannot succeed. As much as we may desire change from the
grass roots, it cannot occur without the vision, leadership, and
support of the executives running the business.

You are the people who must challenge the status quo,
not only within the business technology department but
throughout the company. Here I offer you four questions to
ponder in formulating your strategic plan.

- Is computer technology helping the firm meet its goals
and objectives today, and if left alone, will it do so in the future?
- How is the business technology department perceived

by the user organizations, and how well does it support the users' needs?

• What is the performance of your business technology department? Is their delivery meeting expectations? Is the quality of their work producing the desired results?

• What is business technology's mission, or what should its mission be?

This is where the quest begins. It is through this type of process that you gain insights to formulate your own strategy. This is no easy task, nor something you can accomplish in fifteen minutes. Rather, the amount of time and thought you put into answering these questions will be returned to you in the quality of your strategy. And remember, the goal is to improve the delivery of your business's products and services.

Once your strategy is in place, you must assure that each member of senior management has an active role. How and in what manner only you will know, but this undertaking must be a team effort. Unless everyone is involved and committed, there will be no change. As Musashi so elegantly put it: "In large scale strategy the superior man will manage many subordinates dextrously, bear himself correctly, govern the country and foster the people, thus preserving the ruler's discipline."

### For the Business Technology Executive

Your challenge is even greater than the business executive's, for you have two significant problems to overcome. First, you cannot work alone, so you must have the support of senior management. Second, and even more problematic, you must struggle against the very culture that you helped create. Therefore, the first change must begin within yourself, even before you can formulate a strategy for dealing with others.

I believe this is possible and wholly desirable. In my experience, most business technology executives do not resist change; more often, they simply do not know how to initiate it. This is why senior management must be involved. The reward for success is company-wide recognition as the executive who changed business technology for the better. The consequence of not supporting the change is that you have doomed the entire effort to failure.

You must begin by asking the same, tough questions of yourself that the business executive must ask. And, like the business executive, you need to develop a broader focus. You must set aside, once and for all, any notions that business technology controls the computer, or that your department is the sole proprietor of computer services. Then you must focus your goals on how your organization can help the business be more successful, and what kind of strategy will make that happen.

You have the most difficult job of all, for it is you and your organization that must do most of the changing. But rest assured that from this change you will gain the respect and admiration of the entire company, and you will develop the business technology leadership necessary to lead the business successfully into the next century.

## For All of Us

If we are to get what we need, what we ask for, and what we pay for from our computers, then we must work hard for it. It is a quest that holds the promise of great returns, but it is not without risk. You may not get everything you desire. It is even possible that you might fail. One thing all questers share is spirit and determination, at least at the outset. Often it is this spirit and motivating force that makes the difference between success and failure on the quest. But unless you take up the quest to bring down the embattled fortress in your company, and to restore the lost promise of computer productivity, nothing will ever improve.

To inspire you to action, I leave you with Musashi's nine principles, or the Way of strategy:

1. Do not think dishonestly.
2. The Way is in training.
3. Become acquainted with every art.
4. Know the ways of all professions.

5. Distinguish between gain and loss in worldly matters.
6. Develop intuitive judgment and understanding for everything.
7. Perceive those things which cannot be seen.
8. Pay attention even to trifles.
9. Do nothing that is of no use.

# Bibliography

Block, Peter. *The Empowered Manager: Positive Political Skills at Work.* San Francisco: Jossey-Bass, 1986.

In this book, Peter Block takes a bold look at a newly emerging managerial style in this country which posits taking responsibility and instilling the entrepreneurial spirit in managers and their subordinates. While the tone is positive, the book is far from naive; Block understands organizational politics very well. This work is a powerful companion to *The Embattled Fortress.*

Clark, Kim B., Hayes, Robert H., and Lorenz, Christopher (eds.). *The Uneasy Alliance: Managing the Productivity Technology Alliance.* Boston: Harvard Business School Press, 1985.

This work is the result of a Harvard Business School colloquium of more than fifty business executives and academic experts. It contains ten essays covering various aspects of business and manufacturing productivity, each with an accompanying commentary. As a result, it has a depth and breadth not found in many other works on the subject.

Deal, Terence E., and Kennedy, Allan A. *Corporate Cultures: The Rites and Rituals of Corporate Life.* Reading, Mass.: Addison-Wesley, 1982.

This is the definitive work explaining what a corporate culture is, how it is established in a company, and how it can be managed and changed. If this topic is of any interest to you, this book is essential reading.

Drucker, Peter F. *Managing in Turbulent Times.* New York: Harper & Row, 1980.

Drucker's thesis, that these are extraordinary times and require extraordinary attention, is well taken. He devotes time to such topics as productivity, the knowledge worker, and managing innovation and change. He is both pragmatic and lucid when explaining how to approach computer technology.

Drucker, Peter F. *Toward the Next Economics and Other Essays.* New York: Harper & Row, 1981.

This volume contains many interesting essays, among them a view of Japan, a dissertation entitled "The Bored Board," and an analysis of why scientific management will come back. The central essay is "Business and Technology," which readers will find augments their understanding of many of my positions in *The Embattled Fortress.*

Drucker, Peter F. *Innovation and Entrepreneurship: Practices and Principles.* New York: Harper & Row, 1985.

Drucker brings his study of innovation to a peak in this volume, systematically exploring the seven sources of "innovative opportunity." The author states that management is remaking America into an entrepreneurial economy and society, and asserts that new rules and strategies are thus required. Readers will find this work relates to and augments my discussion in Part Three of this book.

Fishman, Katherine Davis. *The Computer Establishment.* New York: Harper & Row, 1981.

This is the single most comprehensive work on the origins and growth of the computer business. It details many technological developments in language the nontechnical reader can easily understand and also explains how certain practices—many instituted by IBM—came into being. It is insightful reading for the executive who understands that to know where we are going we must first understand how we got there.

Grace, J. Peter. *Burning Money: The Waste of Your Tax Dollars.* New York: Macmillan, 1984.

Grace was chairman of the President's Private-Sector Survey on Government Cost Control, and his insights into governmental waste and nonproductivity are equally revealing for the business reader. You are likely to see many ways your company could profit by Grace's comments and insights in this slim but powerful book.

Izzo, Joseph E. *Charting a Course for Management.* (Rev. ed.). The JIA Management Group, Inc., Red Book Series. Los Angeles: The JIA Management Group, 1986.

I wrote the first edition of this chapbook in 1977 to enlighten senior management about the information systems department so that they might better understand its processes and its function. Much of the material herein goes beyond the scope of *The Embattled Fortress,* which is why I mention it here. When it came time to republish it, I was surprised to see how little revision it needed after almost ten years. We have given copies of this chapbook to our friends and clients over the years and would be happy to send a copy to you upon request.

Kantrow, Alan M. (ed.). *Survival Strategies for American Industry.* The Harvard Business School Executive Book Series. New York: Wiley, 1983.

This volume contains thirty-three articles from the *Harvard Business Review* that provide practical, worthwhile insights into American commerce and manufacturing. Its sections cover such subjects as industrial competence, manufacturing as a competitive weapon, and the factors of production. There are classic articles in this work, such as "Managing as If Tomorrow Mattered" by Hayes and Garvin.

Musashi, Miyamoto. *A Book of Five Rings.* Woodstock, N.Y.: Overlook Press, 1974.

This book, written more than three hundred years ago, is a classic work on strategy and has long been a source of inspiration for me. The thoughtful reader is likely to find that Musashi's Way of the sword can also be applied in the competitive circumstances of modern business.

Peters, Thomas J., and Waterman, Robert H., Jr. *In Search of Excellence: Lessons from America's Best-Run Companies.* New York: Harper & Row, 1982.

This book needs little introduction. Its primary value is as a source of inspiration and innovation for managers and executives who want suggestions about how to do things better in their companies. Like any book that teaches by living examples, these "lessons" must be carefully adapted to your own practices and corporate cultures. But it is still a landmark book on how many companies do things right.

Salerno, Lynn M. (ed.). *Catching Up with the Computer Revolution.* Harvard Business School Executive Book Series. New York: Wiley, 1983.

This volume contains twenty-nine articles on computer technology and data processing/MIS strategies from the *Harvard Business Review.* The articles take a high-level management view and are appropriate for readers from MIS management as well as upper-level and executive management. Topics range from assessing MIS problems to management issues to user issues.

Strassman, Paul A. *Information Payoff: The Transformation of Work in the Electronic Age.* New York: Macmillan, 1985.

Paul Strassman and I share the view that people must manage technology. We cannot improve our business if we simply in-

stall more machines—computers or otherwise. This book is organized into four parts, each taking a different perspective on information technology: the individual, the organizational, the
social, and the executive.

Townsend, Robert. *Further Up the Organization: How to Stop
Management from Stifling People and Strangling Productivity.*
New York: Knopf, 1984.

This volume, a sequel to Townsend's *Up the Organization,* is a
witty and anecdotal guide to improving your managerial style.
You won't agree with everything Townsend says, but there are
kernels of wisdom everywhere. His chapter titled "Computers
and Their Priests" is as true now as when he first wrote it in
1970.

# Index

## A

Accountability: dispersal of, 124; issue of, 26

Ad hoc level: for creative control, 121-122; for systems architecture, 74-75

Aerospace firm, applications expense for, 25

Aircraft manufacturing firm, computer costs at, 2

Applications: complexity and expense of, 25; development backlog of, 24-25; dispersing, 63; evolution of, 29-30; outdated programs for, 25

Architecture: computer, 28-29; dispersed, 103-117, 125. *See also* Systems architecture

Automation: criteria for, 19; islands of, 15-17

## B

Bacon, F., 65

Banks: personal computing at, 45; technology and business planning for, 18

Belloc, H., 124

Block, P., 145

Boyer, B., 48-49

Brady, H., 14-15

Bricklin, D., 43

Business planning, technology planning balanced with, 17-18

Business technology: assumptions about, 34-42; background on, 34-35, 103-104; as business, 104-107; and challenging status quo, 138-143; and change, 117; concept of, 33; control methods for, 118-128; and cost issues, 116; and education, 126; engineering/manufacturing compared with, 105; enlightened users in, 43-53; executive involvement in, 129-137; executive policy committee for, 132-137; future environment for, 115; future systems organization for, 111-115; and mission concentration, 105-106; new role of, 123; and organizing for mission, 106-108; planning, 84-99; present systems organization for, 107-111; as profession, 40-41; as resource, 64; restruc-

151

works, 89-90. *See also* Executives

Level of maximum management (LOMM), and systems architecture, 77-81

Locke, J., 71

Lockheed, skunk works at, 87

Lorenz, C., 145

**M**

McGowan, W. G., 51

Machiavelli, N., 118

Maintenance, issue of, 25, 116-117

Manufacturing firm: executive policy committee for, 136-137; robotics for, 16-17

Mayo, E., 136

MCI Communications Corporation, and enlightened users, 51

Microcomputers. *See* Personal computers

Mission: concentration on, 105-106; organizing for, 106-108

Musashi, M., 139, 141, 142, 148

**N**

Northrop Aircraft, and enlightened users, 48-49

**O**

Objectives, business technology aligned with, 129-137

Olsen, K., 57

**P**

Personal computers (PCs): at ad hoc level systems, 75; background on, 43-44; balanced use of, 45-46; as catalysts, 51-52; or corporate computers, 44-45; enlightened users for, 43-53; idle, 10; and knowledge users, 46-47; and vision and renewal, 52-53

Peters, T. J., 148

Pharmaceutical distribution company, and technology and business planning balance, 17-18

Planning: analysis of, 84-99; "as-is" and "to-be," 95-96; background on, 84-85; business and technology balanced in, 17-18; and goal setting, 91-93; new approach to, 87-90; old techniques for, 85-87; for systems architecture, 79-83, 91-93; for systems organization, 112-113; team involvement in, 93-94; and technology exploration, 94-99; and transfer of technology, 113

President's Private-Sector Survey on Government Cost Control, 147

Product support, functions of, 109-110

Productivity: promises of, 7-20; quest for, 1-4

Programmers, and restructuring, 41-42

**Q**

Quality, issue of, 26

Quality assurance, functions of, 110-111, 114-115

**R**

Response time, issue of, 25

Restaurant chain, information needed for, 13

Robotics, and automation islands, 16-17

**S**

Salerno, L. M., 148

Schumpeter, J., 23

Skunk works: as approach to planning, 87-90; and building business model, 93; and developing systems architecture, 91-93; environment for, 90; goals for, 91-92; leader for, 89-90; team composition for, 88-89; and team

## DATE DUE

| | | | |
|---|---|---|---|
| | | | |
| | | | |
| | | | |
| | | | |
| | | | |
| | | | |
| | | | |
| | | | |
| | | | |
| | | | |
| | | | |
| | | | |
| | | | |